# Welcome

I cannot begin to express how honored I am that you are about to read my book. I have written it in the hopes that you will learn a new skill, self-hypnosis, and that it will transform your life in as many miraculous and beautiful ways as it has mine.

This book shares the tools you need to transform your life from the inside out; I have also created a few complementary resources for you if you want to go further:

### The Website: www.CloseYourEyesGetFree.com

While the next 11 chapters have everything you need in order to master the practice of self-hypnosis, if you would like to go above and beyond, I recommend using the recordings and videos found at www.CloseYourEyes GetFree.com daily as you make your way through this book.

### The Hashtag: #CloseYourEyesGetFree

Join our worldwide community of readers who are learning the power of self-hypnosis right along with you. Choose your favorite social media platform (e.g., Instagram or Twitter) and use #CloseYourEyesGetFree to share your self-hypnosis success stories, your selfies and "shelfies" with this book, or any questions you may have. Please be sure to tag me @GraceSmithTV so I will have an opportunity to personally respond and cheer you on!

### The Newsletter: Grace Notes

Grace Notes are my daily messages to help you to become more positive and calm. At the time of writing this book, I send them out just about daily to over 50,000 people through email. What's the most common reply I receive from Grace Notes subscribers? "This is exactly what I needed to hear today!" I'm sure you'll love receiving them as much as I love writing them. Visit www.gshypnosis.com to sign up to receive Grace Notes for free; these are a fun way to help you maintain a daily self-hypnosis practice even after you have finished reading this book.

For additional resources, please turn to page 251.
Thank you for coming along on this journey with me!

## Praise for Grace Smith and
# *Close Your Eyes, Get Free*

"Grace personally helped me overcome a severe fear-of-flying that left me crying, shaking, and often simply unable to travel for nearly 20 years. In her new book, Grace unlocks the transformative power of hypnosis for people across the planet, debunking myths and giving readers the resources they need to enact real, lasting change in their lives."

—Liz Moody, Food Editor at MindBodyGreen, writer, photographer, recipe developer, creator of EatWell Europe

"Grace Smith works miracles. I was completely new to hypnosis before I met her, and the results we experienced together were nothing short of amazing. I trust her—and the work she does—implicitly."

—Gala Darling, speaker, author *of Radical Self-Love: A Guide to Loving Yourself and Living Your Dreams*

"*Close Your Eyes, Get Free* is one of the most important books you'll ever read. We all have the power to change our lives, and with self-hypnosis, it really is that easy. Hypnosis isn't voodoo magic; it works because it's based in science, and Grace Smith teaches you how to use it to change bad habits and stop negative self-talk all by yourself. *Close Your Eyes, Get Free* makes changing your life so easy that it feels like cheating."

—Karyn Bosnak, author of *Save Karyn* and *What's Your Number?*

"Grace Smith empowers people to rise above their limiting beliefs. Grace's insights on the subconscious mind gives you a soulful invitation to spring clean your past and release the patterns that prevent you from living your best life. You'll emerge from these pages with a fresh perspective on the power you have to create your own reality."

—Sarah Prout, bestselling author, creator of The Manifesting Academy, Host of The Journey to Manifesting Podcast

"Grace's energy put me into a calm, relaxed state, and the guided imagery is still salient in my mind. Working with Grace has truly made a positive impression on my daily life."

—Prince Ea, filmmaker, speaker, activist

"Grace is a passionate healer who's accessible and real. Her down-to-earth approach to hypnosis is relevant and relatable. She's taken an age-old technique and made it a practical tool for modern life. This is the book that hypnotherapy has needed for ages, and we can't think of a better person than Grace Smith to write it."

—Ophira and Tali Edut, The AstroTwins, astrostyle.com

"I had been skeptical about hypnosis but through Grace came to know how powerful and effective it is in uncovering limitations that were holding me back from living my best life. Working with Grace has transformed my relationship with my career, my skin, my self-worth and so much more. I'm always telling people: you should try hypnosis for that! and with *Close Your Eyes, Get Free*, now everyone can!"

—Amber Skye, actress, singer, songwriter

"*Close Your Eyes, Get Free* is a treasure-trove of great hypnosis information for both the hypnosis enthusiast and the professional hypnotherapist. Using real world examples, stemming from personal and client experiences, Master Hypnotist Grace Smith has actually written a treatise on how to live a better, more rewarding, productive, and happier life."

—George Bien, Principal Trainer, International Association of Counselors and Therapists

"In *Close Your Eyes, Get Free*, Grace Smith gives a gift to her readers in easy to understand language of one of the most comprehensive overviews of self-hypnosis. If you are mildly fascinated with the effectiveness of self-hypnosis or yearning to study and become engaged in the field, you will want to read this book."

—Marie F. Mongan, author, *HypnoBirthing: A Celebration of Life* and President of HypnoBirthing International

"Grace beautifully expresses the profound ways to use hypnosis throughout this book that are accessible and easy to implement. I am confident readers will transform by Grace's stories, examples and techniques."

—Erin Stutland, Mind Body Movement Specialist, Life Coach, and TV Host

"It is so absolutely perfect that the title of this book is *Close Your Eyes, Get Free* because freedom is what Grace Smith, in every moment, embodies. This book is a gift Grace is giving to all of us—to learn what she knows, to practice the way of life she leads. Thank you Grace, for being such an example of what's possible for all of us—to show us the way by walking just a few steps ahead. This book is a blessing."

—Michelle Garside and Ali Leipzig, Co-Founders of Soul Camp

"Grace Smith is the real-deal. Her poise, kindness, and wisdom is felt in everything she does. She will give you the grounded wisdom you need to change your life in all the ways you want to. I adore her and this book."

—Katie Dalebout, author of: *Let It Out*, host of: Let It Out Podcast

"Grace's hypnosis has helped me for the past 4 years, from completely eliminating anxiety around food, detaching from negative relationships, and even increasing my financial abundance. In fact, whenever I feel something holding me back, self-hypnosis is one of the first tools I reach for."

—Danny J, speaker and creator of #FindTheMoneyProject

"Grace's book helps break down the super practical sides of hypnosis from anxiety to weight loss. The exercises are simple and time efficient even for a mamma like myself who has a very active 2½ year old daughter. I have noticed a level of ease when it comes down to getting things done that I often find myself procrastinating about."

—Leora Edut, creatrix of Goddess on the Go

"Even the most skeptical of readers will find in this book important information that will serve them well in their quest to changing negative habits and behaviors. Grace's book is a significant tool for two main reasons: first, it debunks a lot of the popular myths around hypnosis and second, it helps you learn how to practice self-hypnosis as an empowerment and healing tool. It will help you achieve freedom indeed."

—Jovanka Ciares, integrative herablist

"*Close Your Eyes, Get Free* offers practical advice on how to meditate with purpose and rewire the subconscious mind, so you can finally have an effective path to change. This book is a must-read for anyone struggling to make a behavioral shift."

—Jennifer Racioppi, astrologer and success coach

"Practical, engaging, and inspiring, *Close Your Eyes, Get Free* is a must-read for anyone seeking more freedom and inner peace. It's the manual for life I wish I'd been given as a child. Grace Smith is able to marry science with spirit and delivers a book that is simply brilliant! Read this book, your life will change."

—Julia Santiago, Women's Coach, Author, Speaker

"Grace and her work have helped me optimize my life and realize some of my greatest business and personal visions. Her work is groundbreaking and anyone who is looking to tap their greatest potential should look into hypnosis."

—Carrie Hamer, Visionary Leader and Founder of Global Fashion Movement "Role Models Not Runway Models"

"What Grace offers in *Close Your Eyes, Get Free* is nothing short of remarkable. It's rare that a self-help book provides such real, practical tools for the reader, and this book does that and so much more. Forget everything you ever thought about hypnosis, and prepare to be surprised, inspired, and healed by this book. It's unlike anything you've ever read before."

—Rebekah Borucki, Meditation Guide, bestselling author of *You Have 4 Minutes to Change Your Life*

"Grace's work through hypnotherapy has transformed thousands of lives, including my own. During a time where I was suffering from my autoimmune disease she helped me ease my pain through hypnotherapy and the best part, it doesn't just work while you're closing your eyes, it truly allows your mind to become free."

—Alexa Carlin, Nationally Renowned Public Speaker, Founder of Women Empower Expo, and Creator of BeAPublicSpeaker.com

"Grace removes any stigma associated with hypnosis by making it relatable, accessible, and meaningful. She channels her energy and passion into helping change people's lives and helping us become our very best selves."

—Igor Volsky, political commentator; Director, @capaction; Co-host of @ThinkingCAPpod; Director, @gunsdownamerica

"If you've thought that hypnosis was just a funny way to entertain a company party or some weird woowoo thing, *Close Your Eyes, Get Free* is about to dramatically change your mind. It's also about to help you start to use your mind to become the best possible version of yourself. Read *Close Your Eyes, Get Free* and prepare to build behaviors and/or quit habits that you truly thought were impossible."

—Talia Pollock, Holistic Health Coach, Plant-Based Chef, Speaker, Podcast, and YouTube Show Host at Party In My Plants

"I love this book and will be recommending it to all of my clients! *Close Your Eyes, Get Free* is a brilliant guide to the simple truth about hypnosis. A must read for anyone wanting to master a calm, positive mind set."

—Dr. Vivian Keeler, Chiropractor, HypnoBirthing Educator, Founder of Amazing Births & Beyond

"Grace Smith is the real deal. I am so grateful that she wrote *Close Your Eyes, Get Free* because her work is needed and now even more people can transform their lives because of it!"

—Nitika Chopra, Talk Show Host, Self-Love Expert

"*Close your Eyes, Get Free* will help provide you with more peace and less anxiety."

—Peter Vargas, Founder, Advance Your Reach

# close your eyes, get free

Use Self-Hypnosis to Relax, Reduce Stress,
Quit Bad Habits, and Focus

## GRACE SMITH

Da Capo
LIFE
LONG

Da Capo Press
Hachette Book Group
1290 Avenue of the Americas, New York, NY 10104
www.dacapopress.com
@DaCapoPress

Printed in the United States of America

First Edition: July 2018

Published by Da Capo Press, an imprint of Perseus Books, LLC, a subsidiary of Hachette Book Group, Inc. The Da Capo Press name and logo is a trademark of the Hachette Book Group.

The Hachette Speakers Bureau provides a wide range of authors for speaking events. To find out more, go to www.hachettespeakersbureau.com or call (866) 376-6591.

The publisher is not responsible for websites (or their content) that are not owned by the publisher.

Print book interior design by Jack Lenzo

Library of Congress Control Number: 2017953703

ISBNs: 978-0-7382-1971-4 (paperback); 978-0-7382-1972-1 (ebook)

LSC-C

10 9 8 7 6 5 4 3 2 1

For my wonderful parents, Joni and George.
If this book helps even one person, it will
be because you believed in me.

# Contents

# Chapter 1

# Freedom Begins in the Mind

## An Invitation

You have the ability to transform your life. To wake up feeling proud of yourself and eager to start another beautiful day. You have the capacity to feel joy and excitement rather than anxiety and dread. To achieve this, though, you likely need a breakthrough. A breakthrough is exactly what this book promises should you choose to commit to it. In fact, from the moment you truly commit to reading this book, you'll begin to experience a shift right away. This is what I want for you! If you're ready to commit, to read all the way until the end, to practice the exercises I'll be teaching you, then you are ready for your personal breakthrough. Let's get started!

## Freedom Begins in the Mind

Freedom begins in the mind. How does that statement make you feel? This statement may cause shivers of "knowingness" to run down your arms and back. It may anger you, you may feel as if

1

your forehead is expanding, or it may elicit no tangible response at all. Take a nice, deep, letting-go breath, and read it again slowly: *Freedom begins in the mind.* Really notice how you feel. Your response to this statement is your jumping-off point for the rest of this book. Feel free to make note of it, and then let it go. You're already off to a great start!

When I say that freedom begins in the mind, I don't mean the mind we're used to hearing ramble on incessantly about everything under the sun. Freedom begins in a place very few people know how to access. A place that is mostly silent, hidden. A place where both our greatest strengths and weaknesses are stored like little seeds, side by side, sometimes showing themselves to us when their branches break through the soil into our conscious awareness. But sometimes, they stay buried forever in a state of potential.

The truth is: Freedom begins in the *sub*conscious mind.

Before we dive into how you can access your own subconscious mind, allow me to introduce you to a man named Alexandre who taught me the true power of what you're about to learn. His experience showed me firsthand just how much freedom begins in the mind. His story forever changed the course of my life, and my hope is that it will do the same for you.

......................................................

## Alexandre

They said he was the strongest, the smartest, the toughest. Every military exam, even the ones where he didn't sleep or eat for days, the heat of the jungle pounding down, dangerous predators around every corner, he didn't just pass them; he came in first. He was defined by his physical strength and his willpower. He rose through the ranks of the naval officers just as his father had done and was on the fast track to the top. He was a warrior.

When he was invited to represent his country, Brazil, as a member of the United Nations peacekeeping force, it was a tremendous honor. He packed up his entire life; his wife, an accomplished public defender in Brasília; and her sweet, fragile grandmother. They went with him to New York City, neither one knowing a word of English, their belief in him strong enough to carry them through the difficulties of life in a new world.

One morning, after months of working with the best minds in war strategy, the call came. He was being sent to Syria for an indefinite amount of time. His wife and her grandmother flew home to Brasília, and he packed for the assignment he had been preparing for his entire life. From the moment the chopper landed in one of Syria's most dangerous cities, Damascus, the attacks never stopped. His liaisons were murdered, his strategies were compromised by spies, and his convoy was fired upon. He had been stationed in the most dangerous favelas in Brazil, and he had led guerrilla teams in Haiti, but nothing had prepared him for Syria.

One afternoon, as he attempted to cross a section of desert from one camp to another, he was trapped. Bullets tore past his team as they attempted to press themselves to the floor of their heavily armored vehicle. He watched as a rebel propped up a bazooka headed straight for his window. His entire life flashed before his eyes right before everything went black.

The bazooka never fired. It wasn't the end of Alexandre's life, but it was the end of life as he knew it. He awoke ten days later in Lebanon. He would come to learn that he had been airlifted there after suffering a massive stroke during the attack on the convoy. As the doctors were explaining to him where he was, he had the strangest sensation. Alexandre realized, "I'm not moving . . . I'm not moving." A look of panic came across his face. The doctor took a deep breath and said, "I'm so sorry; the left side of your body has been paralyzed."

He hadn't moved his left side for ten days, the entire time he had been in the coma, and he wasn't moving now. He couldn't stretch his leg, he couldn't lift his arm, and he couldn't even twitch a finger. Nothing. Alexandre felt a panic like he had never felt before. Trapped. Angry. He would use his right arm to lift up his left to shake it, to remind it how to work. Still nothing.

He realized then that the fear of losing his life was nothing compared to the terror of losing his identity. He didn't know himself. He didn't know his body. For the first time in his life, he felt completely powerless.

A few days later, Alexandre was flown to the Rusk Institute in New York City. His life completely changed. Prior to the stroke, he had always believed in personal empowerment through pain and endurance, not mental strength. But suddenly, mental strength was all Alexandre had. There were moments of pure determination and struggle. He'd threaten his body in an attempt to scare it into movement. He'd tell himself, "You can do anything! You're a warrior! You can do this!" and he'd believe it. Then, when nothing happened for another hour, another day, another week, or another month, he'd plummet back into irreconcilable despair.

During one of these moments, Alexandre's middle son, Bernardo, called him. Bernardo had recently begun dating a woman who worked in corporate America but who had also just completed a hypnotherapy certification. He wondered whether she could come by and conduct a session that might improve his mood a little. Alexandre was so desperate that he would try anything but, truth be told, he was a complete skeptic. Prior to his stroke, he thought anyone who meditated was weak. He made fun of vegetarians. He wasn't at all progressive in his views on medicine or holistic healing. For Alexandre to agree to a hypnotherapy session was proof to everyone who knew him and loved him that he was at his wits' end.

When Bernardo's girlfriend arrived, Alexandre could barely muster a smile as he lay there in the hospital bed. Alexandre looked at his wife who was giving the girlfriend a hello hug, and said, "She looks nervous" in Portuguese, which they knew she didn't understand. In just a moment, she confirmed their suspicions, saying she was a brand-new hypnotherapist, not even full-time, but that she had already had some great success with other clients. It's just that this was a very official setting, white coats all around, fluorescent lighting, and nurses coming in and out. Alexandre told her they had needed to gain clearance from his doctors for her visit, which they had done, and that the medical team had given their consent. This seemed to put her at ease, so she said, "Great. We're just going to focus on improving your mind-set and increasing positivity, nothing too intense or going back to the memories of the war or anything like that." That was just fine with Alexandre.

The hypnotherapist sat down in a chair next to Alexandre's hospital bed on the left-hand side and asked him to close his eyes. She began by having him focus on his breath, and then relaxing every muscle in his body from his head down to his toes. She spoke in a soothing voice, and after some time, counted backward. Then, she made a number of nice statements about his positive mind-set and outlook, but Alexandre flinched. It was clear that he didn't feel positive at all. The hypnotherapist wasn't sure this was working.

At that moment she took a deep breath, and the tone of her voice changed. She became more direct and said, "All right now, Alexandre, bring all of your focus, awareness, and attention to your brain. See it like an aerial view of a city at night. Notice where there is electricity, and notice where there is a blackout. Let me know once you see the blackout." He did.

"Good," she continued. "Now, dive into the center of the blackout. Let me know when you're there." He did.

"Good," she said. "When I count down from three to one and snap my fingers, there's going to be a spark of electricity right where you are in the center of that blackout—three, go even deeper now; two, trusting what comes; and one—" she snapped loudly, and he felt it. Alexandre *really* felt a spark in the darkness.

"Good. Now, imagine that golden spark, that golden ball of electricity traveling down the left-hand side of your face, down your shoulder, down your arm, through your hand, and all the way out your finge . . ." She hadn't even finished saying the word before Alexandre's finger, which had been para-lyzed for two months at this point, moved. His finger moved! He felt the electricity go through it. He felt the sensation as if there was life in his left side. It actually scared him at first, like a loud "Surprise!!!" when you walk through the door to your own secret birthday party with dozens of your loved ones yelling. It was like that—a fleeting moment of shock and terror, followed by an ocean of overwhelming joy and gratitude. He opened his eyes and said frantically, "I'm moving!! My finger is moving!! What do I do now?!" The hypnotherapist looked at him with her mouth wide open and tears in her eyes. "Keep moving your finger!" she exclaimed.

They laughed, and he did. He kept moving his hand, which expanded during that session into being able to move multiple fingers, as well as his wrist.

It has been four years since that day, and a great many wonderful things have happened. The hypnotherapist became his daughter-in-law, his fourth son was born, he was given a prestigious award for his service in Syria, and Alexandre is now a navy captain. He's breaking a paradigm in the navy that physical strength is not the only asset they look for now in leadership. His left arm doesn't have perfect range of motion yet, but he can lift it and move it on his own. Alexandre swims daily, and has been walking without a cane for years. In short, his life is beautiful.

In general, Alexandre is now more open-minded and gentler with himself and others. Most important, though, he practices self-hypnosis every morning and night. Let's be clear: Hypnotherapy did not heal Alexandre completely in an instant. It took time, patience, the care of the world's best doctors and nurses, thousands of hours of physical therapy, and other important recovery tools. It was hypnotherapy, though, that broke through the dense, formless wall of paralysis. It shattered the bleak lens through which Alexandre was viewing his life, and it turned on the lights. In fact, hypnosis turned the lights on so brightly that all of Alexandre's hope, all of his "I can do it" mentality, came back to him with a flash. To varying degrees, it has stayed with him ever since.

That hypnosis session taught Alexandre how to access his subconscious, and in doing so, he was set free mentally, physically, emotionally, and even spiritually. Alexandre will always be grateful for this experience. It taught him the fundamental principle by which he now lives—freedom begins in the mind.

I am the hypnotherapist in this story, which brings tears to my eyes every time I tell it. Alexandre is now my father-in-law, and he shared this story with our families when I married his son, the love of my life, Bernardo.

Alexandre's experience with hypnosis is why I quit my fancy job in corporate America and became a full-time hypnotherapist, much to the dismay and bewilderment of everyone who loved me. "You're quitting your job to become a WHAT?!" But the doubts, fears, and widespread misunderstandings about this valuable tool couldn't keep me away after that day at the Rusk Institute. In fact, the moment Alexandre moved his finger, my entire life changed. I've been obsessed with making hypnosis mainstream ever since.

I'll tell you more about me and my journey in Chapter 10, but for now, let's talk about you. There's just one thing I hope you'll take from Alexandre's story: His triumph can be your triumph.

Let me be clear that one session of hypnosis did not cure his paralysis. It allowed him to move three fingers and his wrist, which had not moved of his own volition, at all, for two months. If Alexandre could break through his paralysis by accessing his subconscious mind directly, and he did, then imagine what the same tool could do for all of the challenges you face. You don't need to be a top official on your way to active duty to reap the benefits of hypnosis. My clients range from those with the intensity and gravity of Alexandre's story to those who are generally happy, such as a sixteen-year-old who wants to improve an SAT score, or a moderately stressed-out mom who wants to overcome her insomnia. What this book will show you is that hypnosis is for everyone, and it is absolutely for you.

What does the power of hypnosis teach us? Freedom begins in the *sub*conscious mind. Nothing external changed for Alexandre the day he broke through his paralysis. He wasn't given a pill, a shot of some new drug, money, a new house, a new spouse, or a new college degree. It was a shift in his mind-set and his subconscious programming.

The subconscious mind is where the following reside:

- Your beliefs
- Your emotions
- Your habits
- Your values
- Your protective reactions
- Your imagination
- Your intuition

Let's call these subconscious inhabitants "the blueprint of your personality and functionality."

For most of human history, we have attempted to transform, enhance, or delete certain aspects of the blueprint by looking in all the wrong places. Willpower, logical thinking, and critical thinking are the domain of the *conscious* mind. The conscious mind and subconscious mind have essentially a one-way radio for communication. The subconscious influences the conscious all day long, but hardly ever the other way around—not without tremendous effort and thousands upon thousands of repetitions. Until we learn how to access the subconscious directly, lasting changes to the blueprint cannot be made quickly or easily.

In this book, you're going to learn just that—how to access your subconscious mind directly so that you can improve, enhance, and delete the areas of your blueprint that you desire to transform. In this book we'll use the terms *subconscious* and *unconscious* interchangeably.

By studying the subconscious mind, you will learn that all our potential, all our power, and all our peace already live within us. Yet how often do we seek external people, places, and things to define who we are and how we should feel? All too often, we give our power away, asking others to fix, improve upon, and take responsibility for our potential greatness, simply because we fail to see just how much we're capable of accomplishing on our own.

Our thinking can ruin a perfectly beautiful day, or it can brighten a miserable one. Someone on a massive yacht sipping champagne as the sky lights on fire just as the sun dips below the horizon can be standing next to the person mopping the deck. Which one of them is happy? Which one of them is in awe of those magnificent colors? The answer is whichever one chooses to be—the one who has trained her or his subconscious mind to think, feel, and react that way! If her thoughts are about her bitter divorce or her ungrateful boss, it won't be a glorious moment. Even if a shooting star crosses the sky, it will still be a horrible night. The external world has zero impact on how we experience life; it's all from the inside out.

The story of how Alexandre overcame his darkest hour by using the exact #CloseYourEyesGetFree process you'll learn here in this book will prove to you, I hope, just how powerful *you* are and just how much you can control the subconscious beliefs that shape your life. Remember, this is not as simple as "Think happy thoughts, and the entire world will transform into sunshine and rainbows." I'm not saying that, and no true self-help expert is saying that. Self-hypnosis doesn't directly change the outside world. As you use this tool, you won't stop wars halfway across the world or prevent the next flood that destroys thousands of lives. You won't stop your husband from having another cigarette, unless *he* desires to quit and uses these tools, too.

In fact, hypnosis doesn't give you control over anything you've never had control over. *It simply gives you a way of accessing what you've always had control over and never took the time to access or train.* We've been asking the outside world to affirm, enhance, and love us while never taking responsibility for our internal programming. This is not your fault, but now that you know about it, it's your responsibility. You've always had the ability to access your subconscious mind, to take responsibility for your emotions, actions, and beliefs, but no one ever taught you how to do it. This book will!

Throughout these pages, you'll discover stories from clients of mine who will inspire you to do as they have done, to close your eyes and get free. You will discover the processes that helped my clients who struggled with yo-yo dieting for years but who, with hypnosis, finally lost the weight, kept it off, and transformed their lives. Furthermore, as is so often the case with rapid weight loss, no new bad habits popped up in the wake of the old binge eating because hypnosis healed the underlying reason for the food addiction. In other words, instead of treating the symptom—and binge eating is a symptom of a deeper issue—hypnosis treats the source of the problem. There are no Band-Aids here, only true, lasting transformation from the inside out.

You'll learn about an executive who used these same tools to overcome a fear of flying and then watched as her career flourished. You'll read about people from all walks of life who eliminated fears and phobias, stopped chronic procrastination, and, in general, found greater happiness and peace in their life.

I learned the power of this tool when I used it to quit smoking and overcame my fear of speaking and singing in public. This led to a stint as the lead singer in an all-girl rock band. I wasn't Joan Jett by a long shot, but playing the grungy Lower East Side New

York City bars where I'd been a patron for years was one badass experience. I can't believe I almost lived without it all because of a subconscious belief I could have overcome years earlier, had I simply known how.

Now, if you're still a little skeptical, I understand. I used to believe hypnosis was a joke. In fact, other than laughing during a high school stage show that was meant to keep us off the road after prom, I never gave hypnosis a second thought until my first hypnotherapy session nearly ten years later. Hollywood has always portrayed hypnosis as mind control or as a way to make someone cluck like a chicken. We'll go over these kinds of misconceptions in greater detail later, but let me clear up these two: (1) If hypnotherapy were mind control, all hypnotists would be billionaires; and (2) everyone in the hypnosis stage show *volunteered*.

Put simply, no one does anything in hypnotherapy that he or she doesn't want to do. When I'm asked, "But does it really work?" I'm tempted to say, "No! Not at all! I've spent all these years teaching it to thousands of people because it's absolutely worthless and a complete waste of our time!" But then, I take a deep breath and smile at how glad I am that I trained my subconscious not to be a jerk (LOL). For the most part, I remember how I felt before my first hypnotherapy session, how my point of reference once came from movies and stage shows, too, and how the lack of understanding about the power of hypnotherapy is due to a lack of education. I put the snark away (mostly) and have taken it upon myself to educate.

Luckily, since the time I embarked on this adventure, the general feeling toward hypnotherapy has already rapidly improved. Hypnosis is more accepted and embraced with exciting new research proving its transformative value all over the world. People, in general, are more open to how enormously powerful our mind truly is.

I stopped believing hypnotherapy was a joke because it not only transformed my life, it transformed countless other lives right in front of my eyes. I knew that if everyone could see the results I've seen, those old misguided stigmas would melt away. Luckily, in just a few more pages, you'll be able to understand exactly what I mean as hypnosis begins to transform *your* life.

## How to Use This Book

This book was written in such a way that it puts you into a gentle hypnotic state and, therefore, will be infinitely more transformative than your typical read. There are sections that are pure information, which will make the conscious, logical mind happy, and there are sections that are intended primarily for your subconscious mind. One of the best ways to access the subconscious is through the awakening of the imagination. In fact, one of the founders of modern day hypnotherapy, Milton Erickson, used long, elaborate, often intentionally boring stories to transform the subconscious mind of his clients.

I have opted to use shorter and, hopefully, more exciting stories to do the same at the start of each chapter. This chapter's story was Alexandre's triumph. Whether you were consciously aware of it or not, simply by reading his story, your subconscious has begun to believe that you, too, are capable of such a profound breakthrough in your life. Although Alexandre's story was a true biography of his experience, all future stories you will read in this book are not entirely biographical; they are a composite of both real-life client stories I was given permission to share, combined with archetypal metaphors to make them even more juicy for your subconscious mind to absorb.

Now I know not everyone is into stories—some people love them and can't get enough, whereas others think they're all just a bunch of fluff—but wherever you land on the scale, please give them a shot before jumping ahead. Even though this is a nonfiction book, give yourself permission to immerse yourself inside each of the stories. Allow yourself to find a piece of yourself in each of the characters. I promise you, these hypnotic stories will help you to internalize all you will learn from this book ten times more than just the self-hypnosis scripts themselves. This is because the stories are actually a hypnotic technique! In short, if I didn't know they would help you transform, they wouldn't be here.

At the end of each chapter is a basic self-hypnosis script that even a beginner can master. This is a wonderful way to begin your practice of accessing the subconscious mind; however, as your eyes will be open, it will be a lighter experience and more conditioning will be beneficial. For an even deeper experience that will yield even faster results, I have created a professional recording of an elongated version of each chapter's self-hypnosis script that you can listen to anytime, anywhere (so long as you're not driving). Simply visit www.CloseYourEyesGetFree.com to access the hypnosis recording for each chapter (see page 22 to learn how to begin), and get ready to relax perhaps deeper than ever before. In a few pages, I'll give you examples so you know what to expect!

By reading this book and listening to the corresponding recordings, you will transform your subconscious programming. The scripts at the end of each chapter focus on areas that everyone can benefit from improving, such as letting go of limiting beliefs, turning down the volume on fears and turning up the volume on courage, trading negative thoughts for positive ones, increasing self-love, and more. If you're not sure which recordings you'd like to listen to first, I recommend going in order from Chapter 1 to Chapter 11. If you're not sure whether you should stick to just reading scripts or just listening to the recordings, I'd recommend both if you have the time, or just listening to the recording if you're short on time. After carefully choosing these topics from the thousands of sessions I've conducted over the years, I believe you'll find that they're all just what you need and are worthy of your time.

I can't tell you how excited I am for you! Your best self awaits you at the end of this book. After a few hundred pages and about a dozen recordings, you'll emerge as a brighter, stronger, happier you. Let's begin!

## Self-Hypnosis

As we continue, I'll sometimes refer to what you're experiencing as hypnosis, hypnotherapy, or self-hypnosis. Generally, I've found that people think of hypnosis as the stage shows in Vegas, of hypnotherapy as a client on a couch inside the hypnotherapist's dimly lit office, and of self-hypnosis as a recording used on your own. But technically, they're all the same.

This is because all hypnosis is self-hypnosis. All of the transformation you experience as a result of a session is because of what *you* have done. The power always lies within you.

Let's take positive self-talk as an example. I'm not there with you in the room, giving you rewards when you think nice thoughts about yourself. I'm not there shaking you or depriving you of rewards when you think bad thoughts about yourself. I'm not physically training you. I'm not really doing anything with you at all, am I? Yet you'll find as you continue reading that very quickly your internal dialogue improves, that you're kinder to yourself and, therefore kinder to everyone else, in addition to many other benefits. Who makes this shift? I'm sitting in California writing this in 2016, and you won't read it until nearly a year later in 2017. Can I take credit for how kind you are to yourself now? A year later? I'm not even there! Yet, tomorrow or even later today, you'll find that you're already seeing results.

All hypnosis is self-hypnosis. You experience the transformation because *you* want it, you seek it out, you spend the time reading this book, you listen to the recordings, and you practiced what you've learned. That having been said, for the purpose of clarity, we'll mainly be referring to private hypnosis sessions as

| | Cost | Speed of efficacy | Requirements for use | Time commitment per session | Avg. # of sessions/ repetitions needed |
|---|---|---|---|---|---|
| Private hypnotherapy session | $$$ | Fastest | Requires a hypnotherapist and a quiet location where it is safe to close eyes for duration of the session | Approx. 1 hour (Specific types of sessions may be longer.) | 6 sessions per topic |
| Hypnosis recording | $ | Moderately fast | Requires an audio player and location where it is safe to close eyes for length of recording | Varies; 10–60 minutes | 21 days of the same recording |
| Self-hypnosis | Free | Slowest— requires most repetition | Can be done anytime, anywhere, except while driving | Approx. 1–5 minutes | 90 days of the same hypno-affirmations |

"hypnotherapy," hypnosis recordings as "hypnosis," and to the processes provided at the end of each chapter as "self-hypnosis," even though they are all truly self-hypnosis. My team and I often receive e-mails from prospective clients, asking questions such as, "Is a private hypnotherapy session, a hypnosis recording, or self-hypnosis more effective?" or "When should I use each tool and how often?" To help answer these common questions, I've created a simple chart to help clarify which form of hypnosis to use and when.

Before we dive into our first hypnosis script and recording, there are a few important things to remember:

**Hypnosis is a natural state. We all move in and out of the hypnotic state all day long. Everyone can be hypnotized.** Hypnosis is more similar to daydreaming than it is to sleep. Some people can enter into hypnosis more quickly than others, and everyone can improve his or her ability to reach the hypnotic state through practice. A lot of people think they can't be hypnotized, but they can.

I don't care if you have a "steel trap door for a mind" or are "type A" or are "hyperanalytical"; you can be hypnotized. Sure, Michael Phelps was destined to be the best swimmer of all time with his perfect swimmer body proportions, but if you swam for eight hours a day and trained as he did for decades, you'd be an awesome swimmer, too. Phelps would still probably leave you in the proverbial dust, but you'd leave most everybody else in the dust.

If you tried hypnosis once, and it didn't seem to "work," that doesn't mean you can't be hypnotized. If you tried to just swim once, and it didn't work out well, you could still learn to swim, right?

So, get ready to jump back into the pool and learn a new practice technique in just two more short paragraphs.

**Hypnosis is simply meditation with a goal:** If you've ever meditated, or attempted to meditate, you know that while you may physically and mentally relax during the practice, you are still very much aware of your surroundings and, especially early on in your practice, you are likely to have thoughts running through your mind. Well, hypnosis feels just like meditation: a gentle, deeply relaxed state where you are still very much aware of your surroundings, where you are in control, and where thoughts may continue to float through your mind during the practice. It's very important to understand that if you continue to think thoughts during hypnosis, you are still "doing it correctly," just as you would be with meditation. If you're a bit intimidated or wondering how the use of hypnosis will affect your life, simply think of hypnosis as meditation with a goal and let all of the silly, sensationalized Hollywood portrayals of this gentle, safe tool melt away. Bottom line is, if you find yourself "thinking thoughts" during your hypnosis practice, you're still doing it right.

For obvious reasons, never listen to hypnosis recordings while driving, operating machinery, or doing anything you wouldn't normally do while deeply relaxed. I recommend listening to these recordings in a safe place, which means a comfortable place where you won't be disturbed.

Even though all hypnosis is self-hypnosis, reading a self-hypnosis script out loud doesn't make you a certified hypnotherapist. Please don't read these scripts out loud to anyone ever, unless you have received training and certification first (from an accredited hypnotherapy school; or see page 251 for more information on the certification I offer). Hypnotherapists, hypnotists, and Hypno-Coaches[1] are trained professionals who are certified to work with clients. The scripts and recordings I have provided in this book and at www.CloseYourEyesGetFree.com are safe for you to listen to in a safe place. It isn't okay for you or anyone else to read them out loud to another person. You wouldn't stitch up your friend's cut instead of taking him to the ER or prescribe medication to a colleague, so please don't practice hypnosis with anyone "for fun." Abreactions (which are the release of repressed emotions) can occur, and people can relax very quickly, which is dangerous if they're standing up. If you read something incorrectly, it could have a less than desirable impact. There are about 250 hours' worth of other considerations that you won't become aware of unless you complete a certification course. If you want your loved ones to experience hypnosis (and I certainly understand that desire; I want everyone to experience hypnosis), buy them a copy of this book, and discuss your own fabulous experiences with them.

**Can I record the scripts at the end of each chapter myself by reading them out loud into a recorder, just for personal use?** As I've already recorded these for you at www.CloseYourEyesGetFree .com, there is no need. Correct inflection is a very important part of a successful hypnosis recording and is something you can learn during a hypnotherapy certification course. For the time being, rather than creating your own recording, simply sit back, and relax with the ones I've made for you.

**Are longer recordings more powerful than shorter recordings?** Most of my clients assume that the longer the hypnosis session, the better. Although maintaining a theta brain wave state (more on this in Chapter 2) for a longer period of time is great in terms of your overall level of relaxation and a longer session can cover more ground, the fact of the matter is that with hypnosis we are *conditioning* the subconscious mind. That means the more we repeat the hypnosis, the more we'll be interrupting old patterns of behavior while creating new neural pathways. We live in a busy world where carving out sixty minutes a day for a hypnosis session might just not be realistic. If it is, fantastic! But I would rather my clients repeat a ten-minute hypnosis recording three times per day than a two-hour recording one time per week. In other words, frequency of use tends to be a great indicator of successful, lasting outcomes, rather than simply the length of the session itself.

**Is hypnosis sleep?** I realize it can be confusing when movies and stage shows often employ the word *sleep* shouted out at the top of the hypnotist's lungs, followed by the slumping-over of the client; however, hypnosis itself is not sleep and the client is not sleeping during a hypnotherapy session. Is it possible for a client to fall asleep during a hypnotherapy session or while listening to a recording? Yes, however, the two are mutually exclusive and if this happens, there tends to be a very simple explanation: the client was exhausted and her body needed a nap! As hypnosis is not sleep, one does not "wake up" from hypnosis; the client simply comes out of the theta brain wave state and returns to a regular waking state of consciousness.

I'm often asked whether hypnosis still works if the client *actually* falls asleep during a session or while listening to a recording. I've found that although most clients like to know what has been said during the session on a conscious level, which only happens if they remain awake, the suggestions are absorbed whether the client is in a theta brain wave state (awake and deeply relaxed) or in a delta brain wave state (sleeping). As the hypnotic suggestions are transforming the subconscious mind, which is fully engaged while you sleep, the fact that the conscious mind disengages through sleep doesn't seem to decrease the efficacy of the session or recording. The only difference is that the client won't remember what has been said.

**Are there any circumstances under which hypnosis is not recommended?** Hypnosis, in any form, is not currently recommended if you have been diagnosed with schizophrenia. Although this is the only condition we as hypnotherapists are trained to always refer out to a licensed health professional, of course, it is always advised that you discuss any new alternative, wellness, self-development, or therapeutic tool with your physician first. As I am not a medical doctor, please know that nothing I have written in this book is medical advice and that I strongly encourage you to discuss your desire to use hypnosis with your primary care physician before practicing any of the following exercises.

## Various Ways to Reprogram Your Subconscious Mind

As we discussed, there are three primary ways to experience hypnosis: through a private hypnotherapy session, a hypnosis recording, or self-hypnosis. In this book I've provided you with written self-hypnosis scripts for each and every chapter as well as longer recordings of the same self-hypnosis scripts found at www .CloseYourEyesGetFree.com.

Hypnotherapy sessions and hypnosis recordings tend to be much longer and more elaborate than self-hypnosis processes, which is why we rely on the hypnotherapist or the recording to do most of the talking. With self-hypnosis, the processes are powerful yet short and succinct so that we can easily remember all of the steps. I have also provided a few examples of full-length hypnotherapy sessions and hypnosis recordings at www.CloseYourEyes GetFree.com so that you can easily compare these three different methods. For now, let's get started with the method that you can practice anytime, anywhere, and as often as you would like.

## The Four Steps to Mental Freedom

The Four Steps to Mental Freedom are a framework for success that I developed after conducting thousands of private hypnotherapy sessions. I came to realize that there is an optimal order in which personal transformation can take place in order to achieve the most powerful and long-lasting results. We begin with what is most obvious—our actions, moving next to what is more subtle—our thoughts, and then into what is working beneath the surface—the subconscious, wrapping it all up with service, which is a powerful antidote to constantly thinking and talking about our issues (which only strengthens them). In hypnotherapy we always begin with the solution, the desired end result, in mind and then sometimes make our way backward into the source of an issue so that we can clean up, clear it out, and replace it with a positive alternative. We'll do the same here in this book, beginning with the solution in mind in Chapters 5 through 8.

# Self-Hypnosis

We have arrived at our first self-hypnosis process. Although there are many ways you can practice self-hypnosis, I have opted for short, simple processes that will be easy for you to learn and follow along with at first, and then memorize over time. While there are self-hypnosis books out there with lengthy scripts you can read through like stories, I have designed our self-hypnosis a little differently. I feel the most powerful part of self-hypnosis is that you can do it anytime, anywhere; however, that requires you being able to actually *remember* all of the steps and hypno-affirmations. If you would like to experience hypnosis that is longer, more detailed, varied, and that is not quite so focused on hypno-affirmations, you can log into www.CloseYourEyesGetFree.com and listen to the hypnosis recordings that are paired with each chapter's self-hypnosis process.

The process you are about to learn is both incredibly simple and powerful; it can cut your stress in half or more. The truth is, stress has become a habit. It's no longer something we experience as a result of a stressful *situation*. We have become so conditioned to experience stress that we feel it as a result of almost *any* experience.

Stress is damaging for many reasons. Primarily, when the body produces a substantial amount of the stress hormone cortisol, the brain automatically operates from a place of fear and survival—two emotions that cause us to be the least open to suggestion and the most shut down. This means that when you're worked up and cursing yourself for having another slice of chocolate cake, you're closed off, essentially unable to change.

A long wait in the grocery store line isn't actually stressful. It's an inconvenience perhaps, potentially even annoying if you need to be somewhere else, but it isn't actually *stressful*. Yet, how many of us have experienced what we would describe as stress or anxiety in a similar situation? So, finally, here's a tonic for every "stressful" situation that will in the short term cut stress by more than 50 percent, and with enough repeated use, will create a new normal for you, one that is much more calm, steady, and balanced.

## Self-Hypnosis Process: 60-Second Stress Relief

I suggest reading through the following directions two or three times before beginning so that you will be able to follow along easily.

- Begin by making note of your starting stress level. 10 = a full-blown panic attack and 0 = zero stress, no stress at all, the most relaxed a person can possibly be. Remember this number.
- Sit in a comfortable chair and place your feet flat on the ground, rest your hands gently in your lap.
- With your spine straight but comfortable, take 4 deep, slow breaths, inhaling in through the nose for 4 counts and exhaling out the nose for 8 counts.
- With your eyes closed, count down from 10 to 1, saying "I am going deeper and deeper" after each number: Ten, I am going deeper and deeper. Nine, I am going deeper and deeper. Eight, I am going deeper and deeper. Seven, I am going deeper and deeper. Six, I am going deeper and deeper. Five, I am going deeper and deeper. Four, I am going deeper and deeper. Three, I am going deeper and

deeper. Two, I am going deeper and deeper. One, I am going deeper and deeper.

- Take another nice, deep, letting-go breath and repeat silently in your mind or out loud the following hypno-affirmations, 10 times: I am safe, I am calm, I choose to be here.

- Take another nice, deep, letting-go breath with your eyes still closed imagine feeling calm and happy for the rest of your day. Pretend in your mind that you can see yourself having a wonderful, calm day until you curl up into bed tonight.

- Once you've spent 1–2 minutes imagining the rest of your day being calm and happy, put a gentle smile on your lips, open your eyes, stretch your arms over the top of your head, and say, "Yes!"

- Notice your new number on the scale (remember 0 = zero stress, the most relaxed you can be) and congratulate yourself on how quickly you improved your state!

Here is a simple summary for the process, in case you need to peek your eyes open at any point for a quick reminder:

- Notice starting stress level from 0 to 10.
- Take 4 deep breaths.
- Count down from 10 to 1, saying "I am going deeper and deeper" after each number.
- Repeat the hypno-affirmation "I am safe, I am calm, I choose to be here" 10 times.
- With your eyes closed, imagine feeling happy and calm for the rest of your day.

- Smile while opening your eyes and say, "Yes!"
- Notice new number on the scale of 0 to 10.
- Congratulate yourself for improving your state so quickly!

For a video tutorial on how to complete this self-hypnosis process, visit www.CloseYourEyesGetFree.com. This is a beginner level self-hypnosis script so that you can get a taste for what self-hypnosis feels like. As we progress through the book I will add additional steps to the scripts to make them more and more advanced.

You may also be wondering why these are the particular steps and visualizations we use throughout our self-hypnosis process, so let's take a closer look:

### Why do we begin with noticing our current stress level?

Knowing where we are starting off helps us to gauge just how much we are able to relax by the end of the practice. I've noticed that about 50 percent of clients will relax 50 percent or more during their first self-hypnosis process, about 25 percent will relax more than 50 percent, and about 25 percent of clients will relax less than 50 percent. Wherever you land on the scale, the more you practice, the deeper you will go next time and the longer the results last. Feel free to practice the process twice, back to back, to see what I mean.

### Why do we count down from 10 to 1, saying "I am going deeper and deeper" after each number?

This is a wonderful, simple way to instruct the body and mind to relax very quickly. The key is to go very slowly. However slowly you went your first time practicing, go twice as slow next time and you'll see even better results.

## Why do we imagine feeling happy and calm for the rest of the day?

This particular self-hypnosis script is about releasing the habit of stress. By imagining the outcome we desire, especially once we are already deeply relaxed and feeling safe, we are creating a network of neural connections in the mind in nearly the same way as if we had actually already had a calm, peaceful day. This mental rehearsal is incredibly powerful in creating the framework in our mind that is necessary to have a calm, happy day rather than a stressed-out miserable one. We'll cover these ideas in much greater length over the coming chapters.

## What are hypno-affirmations?

This is a word I've created to describe what hypnotherapists usually refer to as "suggestions." I found that most of my clients were familiar with the idea of repeating positive, daily affirmations and that the term hypno-affirmation made the parallel between these two practices clear. We are using positive phrases that are easy to remember in order to condition the subconscious mind. Hypno-affirmations are infinitely more powerful than affirmations alone as they reach the subconscious mind directly, without the massive impediment of the conscious mind standing in the way. With this simple self-hypnosis process, you are marinating your mind in the kinds of thoughts and feelings you desire to operate from in life. You are taking time to overpower the mainframe that can so often be negative and reactionary. You are now proactively coding your subconscious to be happier, lighter, more empowered, to be free.

# Next Steps

Excellent! You have completed your first self-hypnosis process!

- Now, go ahead and visit www.CloseYourEyesGetFree .com to access this chapter's hypnosis recording. Pop in your headphones, sit back, relax, and Close Your Eyes, Get Free!
- Using the hashtag #CloseYourEyesGetFree on Instagram or Twitter, message me @GraceSmithTV your starting and ending numbers on the stress scale. By using the hashtag, you'll get to see how other readers are improving right alongside you, plus I will have an opportunity to cheer you on!
- Move on to Chapter 2, and in the meantime, look out for all of the wonderful benefits you're already starting to receive as a result of learning the power of hypnosis.

# Chapter 2

# How Our Habits Were Formed

Jill has big doe eyes. When you look into them, you feel as if you are falling into a portal, transporting you to a place that's deep with knowledge. She also has a beautiful, endearing smile.

She was always immaculately put together, but without seeming to care about her appearance in a self-absorbed way. If a strand of hair was ever out of place, it didn't look messy. Instead, it seemed to spark an air of adventure, rebelling against the rest of the neat ponytail. She was the type of woman who had so many truly close girlfriends that she was a bridesmaid at least three times per year for close to a decade. She was a true friend. When she communicated, she checked in fully, writing a long message. She was somehow completely devoid of jealousy and meanness.

Even though she exhibited a great deal of happiness with everyone else, trouble was making its way through her system, starting in her stomach, a breeding ground for worry. It snaked up her spine and out her mouth, which she would fill with her fingers and then . . . bite. She chewed her nails and cuticles until they bled. She chewed them even though her mother made a face every time she did. She bit them even though everything about her was meticulous and ironed and looked as though she was going out for brunch in the Hamptons. She bit them even though the cuticles embarrassed her to no end. She couldn't stop, and she didn't know why.

She had developed the habit at a very young age, as many people do. She couldn't remember a time when she didn't bite her nails.

At the age of twenty-four, Jill decided to seek out hypnotherapy as a possible solution. A friend of a friend had used hypnosis to quit smoking with success, so she thought it was worth a shot.

On an unusually warm New York day, she walked into her first appointment with her hypnotherapist, Mary. Her hesitation showed because she was almost ten minutes late. She apologized for her tardiness and held her imaginary armor close as she sat down in Mary's office.

Mary smiled to herself, knowing that this kind of body language was common during the first session. It was apprehensive, closed off, and while kind, definitely skeptical. It was in stark contrast to the body language people would show during their second and third sessions once they knew that hypnosis is nothing more than meditation with a goal.

"So, how can I help you today, Jillian?" Mary asked.

"Oh, you can call me Jill," she said, as her body started to wriggle around in her chair a little—a sign that her body was attempting to get comfortable with the idea of sharing her feelings with a stranger. She looked up, and Mary was smiling, waiting patiently.

Jill smiled back and uncrossed her arms before continuing, "Well, honestly, everything is pretty good. My job can be really stressful sometimes, but overall, I really have very little going wrong. I'm not even sure if you can help me. You see, I have one thing in particular that's really holding me back. It might sound silly or small. I kind of feel bad for making such a big deal out of it. I'm sure you help people with much bigger problems, but it does bother me." Jill paused and looked into Mary's eyes. "I've been biting my nails for years, and I can't stop. I've tried everything. I put horrible tasting stuff on my fingers. I even tried wearing gloves. I know it's gross and unsanitary. Since I can't stop, I feel really weak, and that makes me so sad. I didn't think I was going be a weak person."

After another big breath, Jill began to sob.

Mary held space for Jill, letting her know in a soothing voice that the tears were an important emotional release. "Just let them keep on flowing for as long as it feels good to cry," she said.

After a few minutes, Jill took a few deep breaths, began wiping away the tears, and grabbed a tissue from an oversize box on the table next to her chair. She let out a little laugh. "I guess this happens a lot here, huh?"

Mary laughed. "You could say that again! It's wonderful because letting out all of that pent-up emotion allows us to get to the root of this even faster. You see, the nail-biting is a symptom; it's not the problem itself. It's how your system is choosing to cope with something else."

Jill stared off into space and said, "That makes sense, but what is it then? What's the bigger problem?"

Mary smiled and said, "Let's find out, shall we? First you're going to relax deeply. Once you're relaxed and feeling safe, you'll become more open to suggestions, but only those suggestions you want to be open to. In fact, the more you want to be open to them, the more open you will be. Does that make sense?"

"So, no clucking like a chicken?"

"Not unless you *want* to cluck like a chicken, and even if you do, I'm not sure that would be a good use of the money you paid for this session."

They both laughed. At this point, Jill's body language relaxed. She closed her eyes and took a nice, deep, letting-go breath.

Within a few moments, Jill was in a comfortable theta brain wave state—the sweet spot between the beta brain wave, which is fully awake consciousness, and the delta brain wave, which is sleeping.

Mary then asked Jill to return to the very first time she ever bit her nails. All of a sudden, Jill was "Little Jilly-bean," sitting in her kindergarten class. She described to Mary how music was playing in the classroom, and four desks were arranged in little clumps throughout the room, all facing each other. They were supposed to be coloring silently, and Jill was having a great time running her brightly colored crayons back and forth across her paper. All was going well until Julia, the little girl next to her, started asking Jill questions in a loud whisper.

Jill whispered back, "We're supposed to be quiet!" But Julia kept at it. "Why aren't you coloring in the lines? Why didn't you wear pink today like always? Did Mrs. K say we were going to lunch soon?"

Exasperated and terrified of getting in trouble, Jill whispered loudly, "Please be quiet!" A hush came over the room as the squeak of their teacher's chair across the linoleum floor indicated Jill's worst fears were coming true. Mrs. K, not known for her gentle touch, came over and yelled at Jill for being a bad little girl. She told her the directions were simple—to color silently and that Jill couldn't even follow the simplest of instructions. To add insult to injury, Mrs. K then took the picture Jill was coloring and pinned it up on the blackboard. "This is a reminder to follow the rules because Jill couldn't," at which point the students laughed and pointed at her picture, making comments about how she didn't even color within the lines.

Tears began to run down Jill's face as she described to Mary how Little Jilly-bean felt in real-time. "My face feels hot. My heart is beating so fast. I can't really think clearly, and . . . oh my god . . . my hands are under the desk and I'm picking my cuticles."

"That's right," Mary said, "and have you ever done this before?"

"No, this is the first time I've ever picked at my nails and cuticles. I just don't know what else to do. Everyone is looking at me."

The session progressed, and eventually included inner child healing by inviting adult Jill, the beautiful grown-up woman, to have a conversation with Mrs. K and share how this form of public embarrassment had traumatized her. During the conversation, Jill could see with adult eyes how tired the teacher looked, and she was able to feel compassion for Mrs. K, while strongly disagreeing with her teaching style. Adult Jill was able to kneel down next to Little Jilly-bean and tell her how much she loved her drawing, and Little Jilly-bean was able to remind Julia, the little girl next to her, that if she had a question, she should ask the teacher since whispering wasn't allowed.

When the session ended, Jill blinked a handful of times, becoming aware of her surroundings. Then, she sat forward in her chair and said, "I had no idea! I had no memory of this until today! This makes so much sense. I feel so bad for Little Jilly-bean. I can't believe how cruel Mrs. K was to her, to me. But I feel badly for Mrs. K, too. I'm so happy we did this. I feel so much lighter now. I can't thank you enough. I'll be back next week."

Right away, Jill found a dramatic increase in her overall confidence, and her nail-biting decreased significantly from multiple times per day to a handful of times that week. This, in and of itself after one session, was fantastic.

Over the course of five more sessions, Mary and Jill worked on conditioning, a key component to maximizing the benefits of hypnotherapy. Simple phrases, such as *I am safe, I am calm, I choose to be here*, reconditioned her subconscious to be less anxious and calmer. Sipping water was offered to the subconscious as a replacement to nail-biting, and eventually, the habit stopped all together. For months on end, Jill was free from the habit that had caused her so much pain. After a few months, the habit did return sporadically, usually during a particularly stressful week at work, but never to the same extent as before the hypnosis sessions. Jill understood that the nail-biting was a symptom, not the problem, and that if it came back, it was her body signaling a level of stress that was seeking an outlet. Jill now thanks her body for letting her know, pops in her headphones, closes her eyes, and gets free.

...............................................

As I mentioned in Chapter 1, I begin each chapter with a short story for a very simple reason: stories are hypnotic—they help us ease into a focused, relaxed, imaginative state; and we can remember information that we learn while in this state rather easily. I'm sure you can remember the premise of your favorite novel from childhood much more easily than you can the contents of a heavy textbook, and I imagine the stories from this book will stand out in your memory as well.[1]

# Why Are We Creatures of Habit?

"I want to stop. I really, really do, but I just can't." "Even though I know it isn't good for me, I just can't seem to stop." Sound familiar? It could be nail-biting as it was for Jill; it could be overeating; it could be shaky hands while public speaking, procrastinating, smoking, or yelling at a spouse or child when it's the last thing you want to do. It's painful. Saying we're going to stop, *promising* ourself and others that we're going to stop, giving our word, making resolutions . . . and then, nothing. It adds insult to injury and often impacts self-worth in a big way, which, as we'll discuss in later chapters, only makes the cycle more difficult to break.

How did we get here? How is it that the most evolved species on the planet can't just, for example, give up coffee if it makes us jittery, or practice a new language every day for just one hour when it's something we really, truly want to do? It all comes down to habits, and habits live inside the subconscious.

Human beings develop habits by learning to mimic from a very young age. This is the way we learn how to be a human within the cultural context in which we grow up. It's why we have the accent or mannerisms that we do, or why we think certain things are rude. We're very much conditioned to be the kinds of people we grow up to be. Certain habits are actively taught, and other habits are absorbed. If someone grows up watching TV with their parents, depending on what the evenings were like, TV could subconsciously be linked to the idea of love, connection, feeling safe, and being together. Or TV could have been an escape from an otherwise unpleasant or scary experience at home. Strong sensations like these, good or bad, aren't easy to overcome.

The aim of this chapter is to show that you are a combination of what you were told, what you were shown, and what you decided for yourself. Unfortunately, without sincere effort on our part, what we decide for ourselves usually loses out to the others. This is because very few of us come into our own until later in life, if ever at all. The opinions of others are whipping us into a frenzy of following along or rebellion. Yet even rebels act like other rebels; there are two levels taking place—rebelling against the status quo ("the man") while needing desperately to fit into the community of rebels. I have yet to meet a person who didn't want to fit in or be a part of some kind of community. The reaction we have to what others think of us is extremely visceral and is one of the reasons that public speaking often ranks higher on the fear litmus test, so to speak, than death. The fear of being ostracized is worse than death. The fear of being cast out is worse than death. The fear of being forgotten is the same.

When people develop habits that don't serve them or that they don't want, it's always, *always* because the subconscious mind believes it's helping them, somehow saving them and protecting them from something worse. You need to stop seeing your nail-biting, fear of flying, or chronic procrastination as a failure of your character, but instead as a series of neural wires clumped together in a way that doesn't help you. You can become aware of what's happening and say to yourself, "There's a connection in my brain that I no longer want to have. It was built through repetition (or shock or trauma), and it can be unbuilt."

"This habit was built, so it can be unbuilt." Repeat that in your mind along with me. "This habit was built, so it can be unbuilt. In fact, by bringing my awareness to this fact, I'm already beginning to unbuild it." Once you can step back and see this as a construct of your brain rather than an innate issue that you're doomed to suffer with for the rest of time, the emotional charge dissipates.

The guilt, fear, and doubt subside. It isn't necessarily our fault that we developed these habits in the first place, but it's our sole responsibility to change the firing of neurons in our brain if we want to have a different life experience.

Human brain development is created through complex interactions of genetic and environmental influences. While there are volumes written about how habits are created in the brain and how unique environments impact everything from obesity rates to ADHD to SAT scores and more, what we will focus on is how you developed the habits you no longer want. Let's begin at the beginning—your childhood.

## Childhood Development

I shared Jill's story at the beginning of this chapter; what stood out to me was that she actively struggled with nail-biting every day as an adult; however, when she was regressed to the "source" of the issue, it was inside her kindergarten classroom. During the session, it was as if Little Jilly-bean was still sitting right there, her heart breaking as her teacher reprimanded her for something she had not done and then making her art a source of ridicule. All the emotions were as fresh as if they were happening in the present moment, and for good reason.

Under the age of seven, our brain operates almost entirely at the level of the theta brain wave state. When you're in this state, you're pure creativity and imagination. There are no inhibitions. Kids play their imaginary games, dance, and cry and laugh hysterically in this state. They don't care who sees or judges them.

Our mind elicits a number of different brain wave lengths, and though we'll discuss this at length in Chapter 4, let's go over the basics now. There's beta, which is our normal thinking state of consciousness. There's alpha, which is light daydreaming and which allows us to be more creative. And then, there's the theta brain wave state, which is a trancelike state of hypnosis. Finally, there's delta, which is sleep.

In young children, the alpha and beta brain wave states aren't fully developed yet. Imagine a young child in a grocery store, hearing her favorite song. She starts to dance with all of her heart. It's because she hasn't developed what we might call the ego, which comes from some of those faster-moving brain waves, such as the beta state.

Now, imagine a twelve-year-old in the same situation. It's highly unlikely the child would start dancing. Children that age would be mortified if anybody saw them being silly! So, when Picasso said that to be a great artist, you have to paint like a child, he was, in essence, saying that we need to access the theta brain wave state so that our inhibitions are reduced.

> "It took me four years to paint like Raphael, but a lifetime to paint like a child."
>
> —PABLO PICASSO

The theta state is also when you're most open to suggestion. Imagine a child you know under the age of seven years old; they're little sponges running around, soaking up everything they see and hear. Most of our worldview is formed before the age of seven—the way we see ourself, the skills we think we have, what we believe we're capable of, what we believe we deserve, how we identify within our community, and how we identify within our family.[2] I can't begin to tell you how many of my clients say, "I'm terrified of public speaking, and I have no idea why." After we complete a couple of hypnosis sessions, I witness them going back to an early moment at home or in school, like Jill, when someone made fun of them or a figure of authority told them they were stupid.

As adults, we wouldn't necessarily think of that as a traumatizing event, but neurological associations are created at the time they happen. So, let's say you're six years old, and you make a painting for your father on Father's Day, to which he responds, "What's this crap?" It's a traumatic, deeply embarrassing, and painful experience for you and can shape your beliefs about your own ability to be creative forever or inhibit your desire to share your creativity with the world. It might even be a factor in how you relate to other human beings, eventually developing into social anxiety. The way the brain deals with disappointment is a result of these early events in our life.

Now, parents, I know you're wondering if every little thing you say to your children under the age of seven is going to scar them forever. Not at all! Not every moment of every day will have that same kind of impact on us for the rest of our life. It's simply helpful to understand how subconscious programming develops at a young age and to do our best.

For example, a hypnotherapist I heard at a conference mentioned during his keynote that one day his son came home from school in hysterics because someone had broken his toy in half. And it was his favorite toy. He just couldn't believe that person could be so mean.

As a hypnotherapist, he was able to recognize the importance of this experience and see it as a pivotal defining moment. "This could possibly forever define my child's beliefs and understanding about other human beings and how to interact with them," he said.

Some parents might just say, "What are you crying about? Don't worry about it. You have a hundred million other toys," and move on with their day. But taking those few minutes to recognize what could be fundamentally shaping our beliefs for the rest of our life is very important. In this particular case, the hypnotherapist helped to reframe the experience by immediately going out to buy a new toy, which they anchored to the importance of forgiveness. What could have been a lasting traumatic experience for the little boy became just another day. Also, just to be clear, the way to avoid a child's potential negative subconscious programming doesn't necessarily include buying them a new toy! There are plenty of ways to anchor a positive message into the subconscious mind, and in this instance replacing a lost item was a powerful way to do that, but it's certainly not the only way.

## Subconscious Programming: Environment, Elders, and Entertainment

There are many ways in which our subconscious mind is programmed, which can result in habits that serve us, hurt us, or limit us. For the sake of clarity, I have grouped the most common sources of our negative subconscious programming into the three E's: Environment, Elders, and Entertainment. Understanding how we developed our nasty habits in the first place allows us to actively reprogram our subconscious with better habits so that our programming actually serves us in a positive way. The cornerstone of hypnotherapy is the knowledge and ability to weed out what limits us and plant what *helps* us in its place.

### The First "E": Environment

Our environment is one of the primary sources of our programming and can be positive or negative depending on various factors, such as where we were born, what kind of family we had, the customs and norms of our community, and our socio-economic condition, just to name a few. As mentioned, our language, accents, shared agreement on what's rude or acceptable behavior, clothing, and even hygiene regimens are not innate. They're learned through our environment.

For example, my college roommate, Justyna, is still a good friend, and we often laugh at the idea that her grandmother used to lovingly yell at her that she wouldn't be able to conceive any children if she sat on anything too cold. She wasn't supposed to sit on steps outside her apartment building on a cold day, for instance. Justyna was far enough removed from her native Poland to see the humor that I, as a foreigner, saw in her grandmother's old-world belief but, nonetheless, as we inched closer to our thirties, Justyna couldn't help herself. She would laugh as she found herself tugging on my arm, pulling me upward to keep me from sitting on any cold surface. Even when we know our customs are programmed, it just feels right to go along with them and wrong when we don't. Is this because black cats or walking under ladders are *actually* bad luck? No! It's because our neurons were wired to feel a certain way about predominant beliefs found in our culture from a very young age.

## UNDERSTANDING GROUPTHINK

"Groupthink" is the phenomenon behind why groups of people start to think collectively with one agenda or set of beliefs. The goal is creating and maintaining unity instead of being open and objective to various opinions, solutions, or alternatives. The group's actions tend to be unreasonable and amplify their moral rightness and social positions. The individual's critical thinking and reasoning skills are abandoned. These beliefs are usually created in isolation where similar backgrounds add to their destructive thinking.

A horrific example of groupthink in action is Nazi Germany, where the government and millions of soldiers and citizens collectively sought to create a "pure race" for Germany by exterminating everyone who didn't meet their criteria. It's difficult to understand how human beings could turn a blind eye to such atrocities, but groupthink helps explain, and better understand, how the group's collective thinking takes over individual reason and even human compassion.

Cults are also often a prime example of groupthink theory in practice. Maybe some members of the cult feel that something is off-putting or morally wrong, but if they don't speak up it's because they believe to oppose the common mind-set of how things are *supposed* to be would have worse repercussions than going along.

Understanding groupthink adds to the conversation about how we develop our nasty habits and even act in ways that go against our own moral compass.

. . . . . . . . . . . . . . . . . . . . . . . . . . . . . . . . . . . . . . . . . . . . . . . . . . . . . . . . . . . . . . . . .

We have come to understand that groupthink is one of the ways in which everyday people seem to be able to commit atrocities, but we can also apply this same thought process to the development of our more benign habits. By studying groupthink we can more easily understand how a mother who tells her children "We're just not good at math in this family" could result in a family who isn't good at math. Her children may all experience heightened anxiety during math exams and might assume they're not going to get into a certain college due to their math SAT scores.

They might not even apply for jobs where statistics or analytics are required, all because of a subconscious belief that to go against the group, to go against the accepted idea that the entire family is bad at math, would make them an outcast and an outsider. The survival instinct kicks in and even though *consciously* it would make sense to excel in math if possible, the subconscious clings to the familial groupthink in order to be accepted. To the subconscious, acceptance equals survival and we will often act in our own worst interest if there is a perceived choice to be made between fitting in or getting kicked out of the group. A place where this shows up quite a bit is in making more money than one's parents and even in breaking the pattern of obesity in a family.

## The Second "E": Elders

The second primary source of subconscious programming is our elders. Something very important to keep in mind is that under the age of seven, we're nearly pure subconscious, meaning we're open to suggestion with a lack of inhibition. The conscious mind has not yet developed, and we're little sponges absorbing everything. That isn't to say that everything we experience during childhood becomes a habit, but what we experience with repetition and/or during a heightened state of emotion can stick and forever shape who we become.

We'll discuss this further in Chapter 5, but as a quick primer, the same brain waves being produced during a deep hypnosis session (theta brain waves) are what we produce almost exclusively under the age of seven. This means we're in a relative state of hypnosis throughout childhood. It would be difficult to learn how to be human, how to speak, and so on, if we were unable to access our subconscious mind readily. What this also means is the people we perceive to be authority figures during that time of our life (parents, guardians, older siblings, teachers) have an even greater influence on our overall subconscious programming. Jill's story is a perfect example of this.

I was taught throughout my studies in hypnotherapy that approximately one third of our developed habits are a direct rebellion against our parents (guardian or most dominant authority figure in our life), and two thirds of our developed habits are a result of mimicking our parents. We either rebel or mimic, and our subconscious mind doesn't know any different path than to either be the same as our parents or to be the exact opposite of them.

An interesting component of the power of suggestion is that beliefs and habits are absorbed more readily when the person making the suggestion is perceived to be an authority figure. In hypnosis, there tends to be a correlation between efficacy and just how much the client views the hypnotherapist as an expert. This led to the development of "Authoritarian" or "Paternal" styles of hypnotherapy, which included the hypnotherapist employing tools to place them in the dominant position. For example, a hypnotist would ask someone to change the position he or she is seated in or touch the client in a way that shows dominance, or would shout such commands as "Sleep!"—techniques which are ridiculous and unnecessary. Eventually, this method gave way to what we now refer to as Permissive or Ericksonian hypnosis (largely developed by and popularized by Milton Erickson). This method is referred to as the "maternal" style of hypnosis.

This authority figure mechanism is why in hypnotherapy school we are advised to never work with our own parents. Parents would need to overcome a deeply embedded belief that they themselves are the authority figure in the relationship and would need to give way to a new belief that their child is the expert. For example, even if my mother is proud of me for being an expert in my field, to her, I will always be her little girl. Therefore, any suggestions I make during a hypnosis session will be seen through this lens, potentially rendering the session less effective. The inverse is true when we view someone to have a great deal of authority. For example, when a doctor flippantly gives the worst-case scenario to a patient with no regard for the vulnerability of that patient's subconscious mind. "It could be cancer" versus "we need to do more tests right away" still conveys urgency without sending the client into a tailspin that could ultimately result in further health issues simply due to panic, worry, and obsession over an inconclusive diagnosis. Even simple changes from "You may feel pressure" to "This might hurt a little" can change everything. In the former phrase, the patient is prepared for a procedure with words that are relatively soothing, whereas the second option causes the subconscious mind to hear "Hurt, hurt, hurt." Then, the body instantly tenses up. In summary, the way we perceive authority figures in our life, especially when we're children, deeply impacts the development of our habits.

## The Third "E": Entertainment

The third primary source of programming is entertainment, which is really divided into two categories: media and advertising. We're all aware of how powerful and impactful the media can be. However, in the context of this conversation, some of the most common ramifications of the media on the subconscious mind have to do with our devastating self-criticism.

In a fascinating yet heartbreaking study, Harvard professor Anne E. Becker measured the effect of television on cultural norms. As you read the results, keep in mind that television was only catching on in Fiji in 1995 and that a decade before, even electricity was rare. As reported at thoughtmedicine.com:

> The results were startling. In 1995, without television, girls in Fiji appeared to be free of the eating disorders common in the West. But by 1998, after just a few years of sexy soap operas and seductive commercials, 11.3 percent of adolescent girls reported they at least once had purged to lose weight. To illustrate this rapid transformation of ideals, Becker quoted from the 1998 interviews. "I want their body," said one girl of the Western shows she watched. "I want their size." By the glow of television, young girls in Fiji "got the idea they could resculpt their lives," said Becker—but they also began to "think of themselves as poor and fat. . . . [In 2007] Becker found that disordered eating habits were "alive and well in Fiji," with 45 percent of girls reporting they had purged in the last month. (In some cases, they got traditional herbal purgatives from their mothers.)[3]

On the other side of the globe, my wise, wonderful Nana shared with me a similar experience. At the time of writing this my Nana is as bright and beautiful as ever at one hundred years old and I love asking her about what life was like "back in her day." She told me that when she was a child, she tended to be very happy, in large part due to the fact that she wasn't aware of what she *didn't* have. Born in 1917 in Belfast, Ireland, she didn't see glossy magazines telling her what her body "should" look like. Without television, there weren't any advertisements for gadgets, clothes, houses, and vacations to show her all that her family couldn't afford. Everyone wore clothes from the same stores and had the same simple toys. The people who had more lived in an entirely different part of town and went to different schools. So, the crushing weight of constant comparison and coming up short didn't exist for her, and her subconscious wasn't shaped by *lack*. Of course, Nana had her fair share of challenges growing up during extremely turbulent times in Northern Ireland, but the bombardment of advertising leading to self-criticism wasn't a part of it.

Today, the concept of beauty has become askew in a way that's harmful to many girls and women. Most of my weight-loss clients hold themselves up to photos of supermodels in magazines, which have been Photoshopped for hours. Media also shapes what we believe is possible as far as overcoming our existing challenges. Movies continue to portray stereotypes, and we unconsciously compare ourself to them. Luckily, this is all common knowledge now, yet it doesn't diminish how destructive these influences are.

Movies themselves are kind of hypnotic, aren't they? When you watch a movie, you bypass the critical factor of the mind, which is one of the definitions of hypnosis. For example, someone finds a magic potion and drinks it and now that person can fly. The conscious mind would say, "That's impossible! I've never seen someone fly before." Yet you suspend your disbelief and go along with what you're seeing because you know anything can happen in a movie. The problem is that the subconscious mind can't tell the difference between what's real and what's imaginary. It also can't tell the difference between real emotions and "fake" emotions, such as crying as you watch a tragic movie scene versus crying during a real-life tragedy. To the subconscious, your heart is broken, and you're crying.

Similarly, the subconscious can't tell the difference between real and perceived stress. When you're about to be actually attacked or you're simply panicking about getting a report in to your boss on time, your subconscious just perceives it as "stress, fight, flight, or freeze time."

At the movies, you're looking up at a screen, and when your eyes become tired, the rest of your body relaxes. This is one of the reasons that some old-school hypnotists used to use a swinging pocket watch. While watching the watch swing back and forth, the eyes tire quickly, which relaxes the body quickly, making it easier to enter into the meditative state of hypnosis. Unfortunately, the swinging watch was used in so many movies and posters with a creepy, cloaked dude leaning over a starry-eyed waif of a woman that the swinging watch has its own bizarre connotations today. Luckily for us, swinging watches aren't a requirement. Looking up at a diagonal has the same tiring effect. Just think about sitting in church and looking up at the pulpits.

So, during a movie, you're looking up at the screen, and you're in a state of focused attention. A common definition of hypnotherapy is: "a relaxed, focused state of concentration." When you're watching a movie, you're not thinking about the fact that your taxes are due in two days. You're completely immersed in the story. Then, when the credits start to roll, you start to think about all the things you still have to do for the rest of the day. It's almost instantaneous that the hypnotic state is over.

Anecdotally, another example is "highway hypnosis," where we enter a relaxed, focused state of concentration while driving on the highway. Before we know it, we're sitting in our driveway asking, "How did I get here so fast?"

When considering that we're in a hypnotic state, therefore more suggestible, while at the movies or watching TV, it could give us pause to consider what we're ingesting for hours on end. Imagine a six-year-old you watching every movie and television show.

What would you censor yourself from, especially now knowing what you do about the suggestible theta state of that age?

In an instant, we can change how we perceive ourself, how we perceive our world, and how we shape our hopes and dreams by changing what entertainment we spend time watching. What a wonderful, drastic shift there would be in our society if more positive entertainment was developed by conscious creatives. While it may seem daunting to ask this of Hollywood, every time you purchase a movie ticket, you vote for what you want to see. Every time you contribute to ratings by how much and how long you watch a Netflix show, you're voting. Consider the impact these programs and movies have on your subconscious beliefs, and allow that to impact where you spend your money and your time.

The second portion of "entertainment" is advertising, which typically reaches us through the use of media. It's important to recognize the persuasive power of advertising companies. We clearly saw this in the 1990s, when tobacco companies were banned from advertising to teenagers. Prior to the ban, the advertising subliminally targeted teen consumers with bright colors on the cigarette packets, flavored cigarettes that adolescents preferred, and language that teens used. To varying degrees advertisers have always used sex and the prospect of sex to sell just about any product available on the market. Commercials of women, in bikinis or short shorts, eating hamburgers for fast-food franchises or falling in love with men who wear certain colognes are the norm.

This advertising has proven to be successful because it affects the subconscious mind. Does that mean we're being brainwashed every time we see a commercial so that we run out like zombies to purchase the product? No. Again, hypnosis is only truly effective when you *want* the result.

According to *Psychology Today*, "While a surprising number of people today still subscribe to the idea that subliminal advertising can make us do things against our will, that's largely just a myth. Research has shown that subliminal ads and other stimuli designed to influence us outside our awareness can do so, but not very powerfully."[4]

That's one of the reasons that marketing to the wrong person is so expensive. That person doesn't want the result you're promising, so those ad dollars are flushed down the drain. Let's say you reach your target demo head on, but they're still being bombarded by your competitors' ads. Advertising companies know it takes a long time for those neurons that fire together to also *wire* together and make the association that purchasing the product will release the greatest surge of serotonin. It's why customer service is so important. One emotionally charged bad experience causes a new strong neural pathway and a customer lost forever. It isn't that we have to fear making purchases without any willpower, but we reclaim our power when we recognize we're being targeted and that advertising companies want us to feel negatively about ourself so that we'll buy more stuff to fill the void. Buying into their messages about what perfect legs look like in no way serves us. It's time to learn how to Close Your Eyes, Get Free so that this self-criticism stops!

..... THE GOOD, THE BAD, AND THE FAMILIAR .....

The subconscious mind doesn't differentiate between what's good for you and what's bad for you. It differentiates between what's familiar and what's new. Unless we're accessing the theta state as an adult using hypnosis or are under the age of seven, anything new gets blocked. This is the way I have described it to my new clients:

Imagine there's a nightclub. The conscious mind is the bouncer, and the subconscious mind is all of the people inside the nightclub. Everyone inside the club is smoking cigarettes. Someone who isn't smoking, but who is drinking a glass of water, goes up to the bouncer and asks to go in. The bouncer says no. The nonsmoker says, "But I can really help everyone in there. I've read all these books on what's healthy, and I want to share it with them."

The bouncer says, "You don't fit in. You're unfamiliar. I have no idea whether you're going to help us or hurt us. I have no idea whether it would be safe to change what we've been doing for so long inside here, so no, you can't come in."

With hypnotherapy, it's as if we tip the bouncer $100 to let us in so that we can grab the microphone and tell everyone what we know about cigarettes. Now that the subconscious can *hear* us, it can begin to shift and change. Now that we're interacting directly with the subconscious, we can actually change it.

Once we've had our say in the nightclub, people start putting down their cigarettes and pick up water. Before you know it, everyone inside is drinking water. So, from that point forward, if someone comes up to the bouncer (the conscious mind) with a cigarette and says, "Hey, can I get in there?" the bouncer will say, "No, you don't fit in."

You can use the same analogy and replace the cigarettes with unhealthy food. The guy at the door is holding a kale salad. Or the new guy at the door is holding deep, relaxing sleep while everyone inside is an insomniac.

The reason for this is it takes a lot of energy to learn something new. A *Medical Daily* article entitled "How Habits Are Formed and Why They're So Hard to Change," sums it up very well:

"There is a dual mind at play. . . . Our minds don't always integrate in the best way possible. Even when you know the right answer, you can't make yourself change the habitual behavior." Habits are formed after a person has learned something new, like how to parallel park. . . . There's a cue, or trigger, which signals to your brain to turn a behavior into an automatic routine (parallel parking), followed by the actual routine of the behavior (each time someone finds him- or herself in New York City), and then the reward. The reward . . . is the brain's own personal cue for when it should recall the automatic behavior. . . . Once that happens, the brain takes a break. "In fact, the brain starts working less and less. . . . The brain can almost completely shut down. And this is a real advantage, because it means you have all of this mental activity you can devote to something else.". . . If you're not thinking about what you're doing because it's automatic, how can you possibly change bad habits?[5]

Luckily, with the use of hypnosis, we can speed up the process of creating new habits and breaking down old ones. Let's get started with this chapter's script.

## Self-Hypnosis Process: Self-Worth

I suggest reading through the following directions two or three times before beginning so that you will be able to follow along easily. Remember, there are video tutorials and audio recordings available to you at www.CloseYourEyesGetFree.com that will help you to become a self-hypnosis pro in no time at all.

- Begin by making note of your starting stress level. 10 = a full-blown panic attack and 0 = zero stress, no stress at all, the most relaxed a person can possibly be. Remember this number.
- Sit in a comfortable chair and place your feet flat on the ground, rest your hands gently in your lap.
- With your spine straight but comfortable, take 4 deep, slow breaths, inhaling through the nose for 4 counts and exhaling out the nose for 8 counts.
- Close your eyes and imagine gentle roots growing from the bottom of your feet down into the center of the Earth, grounding you.
- With your eyes closed, count down from 10 to 1, saying "I am going deeper and deeper" after each number: Ten, I am going deeper and deeper. Nine, I am going deeper and deeper. Eight, I am going deeper and deeper. Seven, I am going deeper and deeper. Six, I am going deeper and deeper. Five, I am going deeper and deeper. Four, I am going deeper and deeper. Three, I am going deeper and deeper. Two, I am going deeper and deeper. One, I am going deeper and deeper . . .
- Take another nice, deep, letting-go breath and repeat silently in your mind or out loud the following hypno-affirmations three times each: Every day in every way, I love myself more and more. Every day in every way, I am more and more proud of myself. Every day in every way, I am more and more kind to myself. I love myself more and more. I am more and more proud of myself. I am more and more kind to myself. I love myself. I am proud of myself. I am kind to myself.
- Take another nice, deep, letting-go breath and with

your eyes closed imagine being kind and loving towards yourself for the rest of your day until you curl up into bed tonight. Pretend in your mind that you can see yourself thinking positive loving thoughts about yourself, imagine yourself smiling at your reflection in a mirror, or congratulating yourself on a job well done while at work, or gifting yourself a mani-pedi, etc.

- Once you've spent 1–2 minutes imagining the rest of your day filled with kind and loving thoughts and actions towards yourself, put a gentle smile on your lips.
- Open your eyes, stretch your arms over the top of your head, and say, "Yes!"
- Notice your new number on the scale (remember 0 = zero stress, the most relaxed you can be) and congratulate yourself on how quickly you improved your state!

Here is a simple summary for the process in case you need to peek your eyes open at any point for a quick reminder:

- Notice starting stress level from 0 to 10.
- 4 deep breaths.
- Grow roots.
- Count down saying, "I am going deeper and deeper."
- Repeat the hypno-affirmations "Every day in every way, I love myself more and more. Every day in every way, I am more and more proud of myself. Every day in every way, I am more and more kind to myself. I love myself more and more. I am more and more proud of myself. I am more and more kind to myself. I love myself. I am proud of myself. I am kind to myself" three times each.

- Imagine being kind and loving towards yourself for the rest of the day.
- Smile, open your eyes, "Yes!"
- Notice new number on the scale of 0 to 10.
- Congratulate yourself for improving your state so quickly!

In this more advanced self-hypnosis process you may have noticed that the hypno-affirmations become shorter over time and we added the step of growing roots. Let's take a look at why:

### Why do we shorten these hypno-affirmations over time?

For most of you, repeating "I love myself" will be at the very least a slightly jarring new experience. For many of you, repeating "I love myself" for the first time could actually be a very upsetting experience because the pain in your chest that accompanies it will indicate just how much it isn't true. Most people think negative, even hateful thoughts about themselves all day long. To immediately switch that up and begin affirming "I love myself, I am proud of myself, I am kind to myself" would result in the loud blaring of our BS detectors, which is not what we want. Hypnosis can certainly be aspirational but it does need to be at least moderately believable in order to be effective. A fantastic mechanism to begin gently shifting our thoughts is to add "every day in every way, I am _____ more and more." This way the subconscious just has to believe that we are *learning* to love ourself, we are *learning* to be proud of ourself and so on. And simply because of the fact that you are reading this book, you know this is true! That being said, repeating "Every day in every way, I love myself more and more" is a mouthful as opposed to the more concise and power-packed "I love myself." In this self-hypnosis script we begin with what is most believable to the subconscious mind and over time transition into what is both more powerful and easier to remember. If you find yourself having a lot of resistance to these particular hypno-affirmations for increasing self-worth, stick with the "Every day in every way, I am . . . more and more" version until you feel comfortable with them, and only then move on to the more concise version. Eventually you'll be able to look yourself in the mirror and say out loud, "I love you exactly as you are" without flinching, knowing you mean it, and having your subconscious support you in that powerful belief.

### Why do we imagine gentle roots growing from the bottom of our feet down into the center of the Earth?

I find that the vast majority of my clients spend countless hours on the phone and in front of brightly lit computer or tablet screens, shuttling between home and the office day after day, with very little time spent outdoors, connecting to nature. Simply walking on grass can have a very grounding, calming effect on our nervous system, and what's the next best thing to actually getting outside and digging our toes into the ground? Imagining it! Those roots are simply sending a similar message to our brain to relax that we would experience if we were genuinely outdoors. This imagery connects us to nature, and grounds us in a lovely, calming way that facilitates an even deeper experience of the theta state.

## Next Steps

Excellent! You have completed your self-hypnosis process for increasing self-worth!

- Now, go ahead and visit www.CloseYourEyesGetFree
  .com to access this chapter's longer hypnosis recording.
  Pop in your headphones, sit back, relax, and Close Your
  Eyes, Get Free.
- After you listen to the recording, please let me know
  how it went! Using the hashtag #CloseYourEyesGetFree
  on Instagram or Twitter, message me @GraceSmithTV
  your starting and ending numbers on the stress scale.
  By using the hashtag, you'll get to see how other readers
  are improving right alongside you, plus I will have an
  opportunity to personally cheer you on!
- Move on to Chapter 3 and continue to look out for all of
  the wonderful benefits you're already starting to receive
  as a result of learning the power of hypnosis.

# Chapter 3

# The History of Hypnosis

The year is 1863. George is a medical student and is extremely proud of his chosen profession. He believes the advancements he is experiencing during his age, during his prime, will make history. Every day, George feels blessed to sit inside the auditorium with his contemporaries. He hears the best minds speak, and watches them perform procedures, and he occasionally asks questions as the procedures are taking place. There's nothing quite like it. While the seats may be worn, stiff, and uncomfortable, George hardly notices.

The room itself is quite cold. George wears a coat and gloves with the fingertips cut off so that he can write as quickly as possible. He leans in as if the closer he can get, the more details he will remember. Every day, he learns more about the fascinating composite of parts that is the human body. He learns about the electric nature of the brain, he sees how far humanity has come in our understanding, and he discovers how much we still don't know.

Today, though, what George saw was truly astounding. A guest lecturer was asked to demonstrate the power of the mind. They joked about it, George and his friend Ryan, while finishing off their cigarettes on the oval before entering class. "The power of the mind" seemed a redundant phrase to them, even laughable.

The mind itself is only power. It's simply unlimited potential. Still, for all of their jokes, they'd never miss a class.

The lecturer began by explaining that his patient was allergic to the anesthesia that had become popular in recent years. The patient was in need of surgery to remove a tumor. George and his classmates braced themselves for what would ensue. They had all seen a number of surgeries without anesthesia as it was not always easy to come by. The screams were not easily forgotten.

Then, the most peculiar thing began to happen. The lecturer began to speak to the patient in a slow, monotone voice, quite different from that of his natural speaking cadence. He began telling the patient to relax deeply all parts of the body. He then told the patient that his eyes were tired, and they would not open, no matter how hard he tried. George watched as the patient attempted to open his eyes. He saw the patient try his damnedest as his eyebrows rose, creating visible creases, yet the eyes remained closed. There was a whisper running through the auditorium. The lecturer continued; he lifted the patient's arm, and as he let it go, he said, "Even deeper now." The arm dropped down with a heavy thump into the patient's lap, like a wet towel. It almost appeared as if the patient were in a very deep sleep, but the lecturer asked him to share with us how he was feeling. And he spoke! The patient said, "Calm . . . light." The lecturer said, "Very good. You're doing very well."

He then told the patient that there was a dial inside his body, specifically where the surgery would take place. He gently pressed that point on the body and told the patient that he could turn the dial from ten, which would be 100 percent full sensation, all the way down to zero, where he would feel nothing. The lecturer then moved the patient's hand over to a small pad of paper on the table beside the hospital bed. He placed a pen in the patient's hand and asked him to write his level of sensation. The lecturer counted from ten to zero slowly, pressing the same spot, as the patient wrote each number on the pad until he reached that level of sensation. When he reached the level of zero, the lecturer asked the patient whether he could feel the pressure. He wrote "o" again. Then, George and his classmates all arose to their feet and cheered. The patient did not move a muscle, despite our noise.

The lecturer made an incision, and the patient did not flinch. When asked his level of sensation, he wrote "1." The entire surgery took place without anesthesia! The tumor was removed, and the patient continued to breathe peacefully. The highest number the patient ever wrote was a "3," but on the whole, he mostly maintained a level of zero to one. George was astonished! After the stitches were sewn, the patient was then brought back to total awareness. The lecturer counted from zero up to ten, and the patient opened his eyes. And of all things, he smiled. He was asked to explain what the procedure had been like for him. He said he could feel the discomfort at the point of incision at about a level five, but during the surgery itself, it never reached above a three. He said the entire time that he knew he was in the room being watched by all of the students, but that it just didn't seem to matter much. Instead, he imagined he was on the beach, as the lecturer had told him to do. He somehow was both on the beach with his feet in the ocean, while also being watched by a room full of students. He was deeply relaxed and felt relatively peaceful at all times. After resounding cheers, congratulations, and thanks, the patient was wheeled into a recovery room.

The lecturer remained behind to answer questions. George then learned he was a physician who had been introduced to the "power of the mind," as he calls it, while treating soldiers on the front line. He was head of surgery at an outfit that ran out of anesthetic supply for more than two weeks. It was rumored that a local man in a nearby village was trained in the "art of the mind" and that he could train people to decrease pain levels in their own body. The surgeon studied with this man, and together, they used this process in hundreds of surgeries moving forward. In fact, the recovery rates of the men were found to be faster than *with* the use of anesthesia. As a result, even once his anesthesia supplies had been refilled, the surgeon opted to continue with this procedure over the others.

He urged George and his classmates to study the mechanisms of deep relaxation, focused concentration, and the power of suggestion. He told them they needed to understand that the pain centers of their clients are located in their minds. In fact, their entire perception of reality is found within the mind, and by harnessing these centers, they can accomplish what was never thought possible. Needless to say, George was thrilled that he and his contemporaries witnessed this powerful tool—"hypnosis" the surgeon called it—and that all medicine would now and forever be informed by the power of the mind.

## The Evolution of Hypnotherapy

This story is loosely based on what I imagine it must have been like for hypnosis pioneer James Braid as he watched the presentation by Charles Lafontaine at the Manchester Athenaeum, on Saturday, November 13, 1841, which pivoted his career focus to hypnosis for the rest of his life.[1] Braid and many of his contemporaries believed that hypnosis would become a cornerstone of medicine during their lifetime. Sadly, and for many of the reasons we will discuss in this chapter, that clearly was not the case.

Even though it has been 175 years since James Braid sat in that lecture hall, hypnosis is still not a cornerstone of medicine, nor is it yet a mainstream stand-alone healing practice; however, during just the years that I have been a hypnotherapist, I have noticed that the use of hypnotherapy has begun to expand rapidly. More and more physicians and dentists are using hypnosis in their offices. The popular BBC documentary *Science of Hypnosis*[2] filmed a live teeth extraction and implant placement with no anesthetic, just hypnosis; and *Oncology Nurse Advisor* reports the increasing use of hypnosis in cancer treatment.[3] Fortune 500 companies are bringing in HypnoCoaches for their top executives, and reality TV shows are producing episodes where lead talent overcome adversity with the use of hypnosis. While hypnotherapy is finally experiencing the boom its efficacy should have always warranted, this is by no means a new tool, nor is it the first time hypnosis experienced popularity. My hope is that by my sharing with you the history and efficacy of hypnosis through the ages, you will be even more inspired to continue using hypnosis in your daily life.

The textbook *Hypnosis and Communication in Dental Practice* provides a wonderful summary of the history of hypnosis and tells us that this tool actually dates back to ca. 1550 B.C. in the Egyptian Ebers Papyrus, an ancient medical text, which tells us that powerful suggestions were read to deeply relaxed patients inside the "Temples of Sleep." Who wouldn't want a day pass to the Temples of Sleep? While they sound absolutely dreamy, this is not exactly where locals went to take a nap, but instead where they would relax deeply and receive suggestions that were considered to be medicinal. Sound familiar?

During this same time in history, the Romans also began building temples for similar "sleep" rituals. My ancestors, the Celtic Druids, who inhabited what are now Ireland, Scotland,

Wales, and Great Britain, had their own Druidic healing rituals specifically for their version of "sleep" temples. So, I guess this "talking to people with their eyes closed" thing runs in the family.

We now know that "sleep temples" existed in multiple locations throughout the world at the same time in history and that the results their patrons experienced were so powerful that their healing impact is known even today. So, what happened? As Christianity started to spread throughout Europe, sleep temples, along with a multitude of other natural healing techniques, quickly became regarded as witchcraft and were outlawed. *The Handbook of Contemporary Clinical Hypnosis* explains what happened in the following way, "With the rise of Christianity healing was seen as a miracle or a gift from God, trance states as evil and practiced by witches and illness and suffering as part of humankind's payment for being born with original sin—just punishment for wrongdoing." . . . "In medieval times in the western world there was a resurgence of the belief that mental illness was linked with demonic possession, and the afflicted would be required to undergo ritual exorcism or tortured to expel the demons involved."[4] In short, the Church unleashed a smear campaign ensuring that there would only be one source of miraculous healing in town. Sadly, this was the start of a centuries-long public relations battle that hypnotherapy historically lost, at least until recent history. And if I have anything to say about it, the truth about hypnosis will once and for all replace the lies conjured up during these manipulative times.

For hundreds of years, the techniques used in ancient sleep temples were unknown to the general public, but a resurgence began in the 1700s. Franz Anton Mesmer (1734–1815), from whom the word *mesmerize* was derived, began using tools similar to what were described in the ancient sleep temples to great effect.

However, as time went on, his practices expanded to include bizarre dramatics such as wearing a black cloak during his presentations and tying up his clients with ropes. The Church eventually declared that mesmerism was also part of the occult. However, as we've discussed, hypnosis is a natural state that we enter into and out of all day long. It doesn't require a swinging watch, a fancy cloak, or a rope for it to work.

The term *hypnosis* wasn't coined until 1843 by Scottish physician James Braid. Unfortunately, from the very beginning, the word has been a misnomer and has added to the misunderstanding of this tool. Hypnos was a god in Greek mythology. He was the physical personification of sleep, so from the very beginning, the deeply relaxed and peaceful state reached through hypnosis was confused with actual sleep.

## Hypnosis: The First Anesthesia

Anesthesia was first used during surgery in 1846. Before the advent of anesthesia, it was a common practice in the medical field to use hypnosis during surgical and dental procedures throughout Europe. John Elliotson (1791–1868), an English professor of medicine, claimed to have performed over four hundred successful operations on patients with the use of hypnosis. Amputations under hypnosis were common during World War I (1914–1918), as well as many dental extractions and surgeries, including the removal of tumors.[5] Hypnosis was also used to treat soldiers suffering from shell shock resulting from that war. Unfortunately this was not so that they could heal and return to a normal life, but so that they could return quickly to the battlefield. While the motive may not have been the most admirable, it's exciting to know that hypnosis was being used in the aid of PTSD patients as early as World War I.

James Braid, who inspired our opening story, published a book in 1843 called *Neurypnology or the Rationale of Nervous Sleep*, which cemented the word *hypnosis* in the medical field. He had been performing successful surgeries and dental extractions for years with hypnosis as his sole form of anesthesia. He was a pioneer who was one of the first doctors to "recognize that hypnosis was brought about by focus of attention and heightened suggestibility."[6]

This was the beginning of modern-day hypnotherapy.

Other medical doctors of this time were exploring hypnotherapy, including Pierre Janet, a doctor who worked at the Pitié-Salpêtrière hospital in Paris. He "developed a theory of dissociation, proposing that in hypnosis the conscious mind becomes suppressed, allowing the unconscious mind to surface."[7]

Around this same time of the late 1880s, Sigmund Freud became interested in studying hypnosis with Dr. Jean-Martin Charcot, who also worked at Pitié-Salpêtrière. Dr. Charcot was studying with Dr. Ambroise-Auguste Liébeault and Professor Hippolyte Bernheim.

Freud was all but moved to tears the first time he sat in the audience of a medical hypnosis presentation. He wrote, "With the idea of perfecting my hypnotic technique, I made a journey to Nancy in the summer of 1889 and spent several weeks there. I witnessed the moving spectacle of old Liébeault working among the poor women and children of the labouring classes. I was a spectator of Bernheim's astonishing experiments upon his hospital patients, and I received the proudest impression of the possibility that there could be powerful mental processes which nevertheless remained hidden from the consciousness of men."[8] This resulted in Freud's using hypnosis as his inspiration for his regression technique known as "the talking cure," which uncovered patients' suppressed memories.

## Stage Act Versus Hypnotherapy

Medical demonstrations of hypnosis, such as the ones described in the story at the start of this chapter and by Freud, were commonplace in the 1800s. Eventually, these gave way to the use of hypnosis on a very different kind of stage. In my opinion, stage hypnosis has done as much to damage the image of hypnosis as the early Church. While I understand how humorous these shows can be and that laughter is healing in and of itself, the view of hypnosis presented in these shows creates a false and distorted idea of how it works. It makes the volunteer look like a victim succumbing to the hypnotist's will, and that image couldn't be further from the truth. More important, it skews the positive benefits that hypnosis produces within a clinical environment.

This section is probably going to upset a lot of my colleagues who are fabulous stage hypnotists and who always incorporate healing into their stage shows. A lot of stage hypnotists have great intentions, and if you just hired one for your next off-campus retreat, you're probably going to have a wonderful time, as many of them do genuinely care about helping their audiences. Still, I believe the following needs to be said.

I love to laugh. When I want to relax or feel better, I often turn to YouTube and binge-watch Grace Helbig for way too long, or I embark upon the bliss of rewatching *30 Rock* until it so cruelly and abruptly ends in the middle of the seventh season. The jokes of my favorite comedians don't hurt us. Sure, Grace Helbig, Jon Stewart, Kathleen Madigan, and Tina Fey may hit us in a place that causes us to squirm, but they don't hurt us in the sense that they don't distort a tool that heals bones faster, stops the leading cause of lung cancer and emphysema in its tracks, and sets people free from lifelong phobias.

The Church hasn't officially condemned hypnosis for about a century, so few people are avoiding it due to the sermon they heard last Sunday. It's because of stage hypnosis and how the tool is portrayed in the media. This is what has caused people to equate one of the most powerful tools for healing with clucking chickens. People who could have quit smoking years ago haven't because they believe hypnosis is mind control, due to such movies as *Now You See Me 2*. They are told in such films as *Office Space* that when they go into a state of hypnosis, they will never come out. *Shallow Hal* attempted to teach us that hypnosis can make one see all overweight women as thin. And the most heinous and upsetting example to date, the movie *Get Out*, had me in tears inside the theater while I witnessed such a horrific and false presentation of hypnosis even as late as the year 2017.

I honestly cannot believe there hasn't been a class-action lawsuit yet to stop producers and screenwriters from the lazy and irresponsible use of hypnosis to explain why a character is behaving in a way they normally wouldn't. Imagine if *every single time* a chiropractor were depicted in a movie they were seen crushing the bones of a patient, it would absolutely negatively impact the world's view of the entire field of chiropractics and less people would be seeking out adjustments that could possibly bring them relief. Well, every *single* time hypnosis is depicted in a film or on a Vegas stage show, it is represented in a false, negative, and creepy way, and as a result, people who could have been free from the problems that plague them continue to suffer. Clearly, I'm sick of it.

Often when I share this sentiment online, I receive some criticism telling me to relax because, "I know it's just a movie, I know it's not real!" And, be that as it may, even if the viewer doesn't actually believe hypnosis does these things and they realize this is all a device being amplified for the purpose of "entertainment," it certainly doesn't give the impression that hypnosis can help them overcome their fear of speaking in public, or that it will increase the likelihood of survival by two times for breast cancer patients. After someone watches *Get Out*, what is the likelihood that they will even bother to see whether the insomnia they've suffered for years could be *cured* in a matter of hours? Mainstream media has skewed the regular movie-goer's possibility of even considering such a positive, potential outcome.

I'm not claiming that hypnotherapy can help everyone on the planet with every issue 100 percent of the time. It isn't magic, and results vary just as with most health and wellness treatments of any kind. But to negate the power of this tool altogether is just as harmful as dismissing the power of Alcoholics Anonymous even if only a percentage of participants maintain sobriety. The people who don't relapse find true freedom. Not everyone who experiences an adjustment with a chiropractor or a session with an acupuncturist can claim it was life-changing, but there are those who have treatments like these regularly and swear by them. Essentially, like anything worthwhile, hypnosis works if you work it and more people will "work it" if they're being told the truth about its potential use in their life, versus the nonsensical display perpetuated by stage hypnotists and Hollywood.

I recently was asked to hypnotize a reality TV star on a *Kardashians*-esque show. While speaking with the producer, he kept mentioning that he would like to make the scene a little more visual. Could we expose the client to her phobia so that we could watch her freak out? Could I give her a cue after the session so that she would do something bizarre without realizing it? Could I make it so that she would forget the entire session, but all of sudden be over the phobia and not know why? How could we make it more "interesting for the audience," a.k.a. more dramatic and better for ratings? I had to explain to the producer that we were fundamentally at odds. His job is to make sure people watch the show because it's shocking. My job, as I see it, is a vendetta against all of the gimmicks that make hypnosis such a popular device in Hollywood movies. Although it's my mission to make hypnosis mainstream, and media exposure is a great way to reach the masses, I had to turn the show down. Luckily, only a few months later I was invited to help a woman overcome her sugar addiction on CBS's hit show *The Doctors*, and that experience was a wonderful way to share with a massive audience just how natural, normal, and powerful hypnosis can be. I am very grateful to the *The Doctors* for portraying hypnosis in such a positive light.

The fact of the matter is that clinical hypnosis is actually fairly boring to watch. There's nothing exceptionally visually interesting about it. That's because it's simply meditation with a goal. I understand the allure and convenience of using a tool in a script that allows the audience to think to itself, "That character would never do that, but he was hypnotized. So, I'm going to suspend my disbelief and continue to watch the movie without questioning the plot." However, perpetuating the ideas about hypnosis put forth in Hollywood and stage hypnosis actively hurts the audience because it causes viewers not to consider a viable option that could drastically improve their lives. Once I saw Alexandre break through his paralysis, I came to find stage hypnosis upsetting and not remotely worth the laughs.

Now that we're all clear on my opinion of stage hypnosis, let's discuss what stage hypnosis actually *is*. Stage hypnotists conduct a number of "suggestibility tests" to find out which people in the audience are a little bit suggestible, a good amount suggestible, or whether they are natural somnambulists. The hypnotists remember who those people are so that when they ask for volunteers, they only bring to the stage those people who were at least moderately suggestible. The key point to remember here is that they ask for *volunteers*—people who already know they will be asked to do ridiculous things and are okay with this prospect in advance.

Then, throughout the show, the hypnotist removes the people from the stage who are not accepting the suggestions so that by the end of the show, all you're watching is someone of a high level of suggestibility who wants to comply with the suggestions he or she is being given.

Now that you understand that people clucking like chickens are only doing it because they want to, let me step down from my rather large stage hypnosis soapbox and introduce you to one of the greatest hypnotherapists of all time.

## Contemporary Practice

Milton Erickson (1901–1980) is a hero to many hypnotherapists. Although he is the father of modern-day hypnotherapy, Ericksonian hypnosis is, interestingly enough, known as being "maternal" in nature, as compared to the "paternal" authoritarian hypnosis of the past. A domineering man screaming "Sleep!" at the top of his lungs gave way to Erickson's "You may notice you have already begun to relax."

Erickson studied psychology and psychiatry, and he competently wrote about "trance induction, experimental work exploring the possibilities and limits of the hypnotic experience, and investigations of the nature of the relationship between hypnotist and subject."[9]

The legitimacy of clinical hypnosis began to take root in the modern medical field with such figures as Erickson sharing positive data and leading the way with his cutting-edge techniques. Ericksonian technique includes a lot of storytelling, the use of archetypes, and supporting the client as they come to their own insights and conclusions. Rather than the hypnotist doing something *to* or *for* the client, in Ericksonian hypnosis, the client and hypnotherapist learn and discover together as the client heals him- or herself. This is the kind of gentle, subtle, and yet powerful hypnosis that's making its way into the mainstream.

In 1958, the American Psychological Association established a certifying board of examiners in both clinical and experimental hypnosis. Ten years later in 1968, the British Society of Medical and Dental Hypnosis was established.

A few of today's key figures of contemporary hypnotherapy include superstar hypnotherapists Marie "Mickey" Mongan (the founder of HypnoBirthing), Dr. Herbert Spiegel, Dr. David Spiegel, Wendi Fressien, Steve G. Jones, and Paul McKenna, who have reached millions with their studies, books, and recordings and paved the way for many of us at a time when hypnotherapy was considered far more bizarre than it is now. Other contemporary hypnotherapists I've had the pleasure to work and study with personally include Paul Aurand, Sophia Kramer, Dr. Vivian Keeler, Sarojini Alva Changkakoti, Randi Light, Martin Peterson, Dr. Shelley Stockwell-Nicholas, and George Bien, to name a few. While each one of these hypnotherapists has a unique practice and may hold views that are very different from what I've written here, without them and dozens more, we wouldn't be in the position we are now to welcome hypnosis into the mainstream. I'm standing on the shoulders of hypno-giants, and I'm grateful. Speaking of gratitude, let's move on to this chapter's self-hypnosis process.

## Self-Hypnosis Process: Infinite Gratitude

I suggest reading through the following directions two or three times before beginning so that you will be able to follow along easily. Remember, there are video tutorials and audio recordings available to you at www.CloseYourEyesGetFree.com that will help you to become a self-hypnosis pro in no time at all.

- Begin by making note of your starting stress level. 10 = a full-blown panic attack and 0 = zero stress, no stress at all, the most relaxed a person can possibly be. Remember this number.
- Sit in a comfortable chair and place your feet flat on the ground, rest your hands gently in your lap.
- With your spine straight but comfortable, take 4 deep, slow breaths, inhaling through the nose for 4 counts and exhaling out the nose for 8 counts.

- Close your eyes and imagine gentle roots growing from the bottom of your feet down into the center of the Earth, grounding you.
- Bring all of your focus and awareness and attention to the palms of your hands. Perhaps you can feel your palms tingling, perhaps you can feel your heartbeat in your hands, perhaps you notice a sensation of expansion in your hands. Just notice and breathe for a few moments (you can choose whatever length of time feels best, about 30 seconds is my personal favorite).
- With your eyes closed, count down from 10 to 1, saying "I am going deeper and deeper" after each number: Ten, I am going deeper and deeper. Nine, I am going deeper and deeper. Eight, I am going deeper and deeper. Seven, I am going deeper and deeper. Six, I am going deeper and deeper. Five, I am going deeper and deeper. Four, I am going deeper and deeper. Three, I am going deeper and deeper. Two, I am going deeper and deeper. One, I am going deeper and deeper . . .
- With your eyes closed, repeat the following hypno-affirmations silently in your mind or out loud, 10 times: I am grateful for _____ (choose a person). I am grateful for _____ (choose a place). I am grateful for _____ (choose a body part).
- Take another nice, deep, letting-go breath and with your eyes closed imagine experiencing immense gratitude for the rest of your day until you curl up into bed tonight. Allow that gratitude to consume you as you vividly imagine yourself hugging and high-fiving and laughing

with all of the people, places, and things you are grateful for.

- Once you've spent 1–2 minutes imagining the rest of your day filled gratitude, put a gentle smile on your lips.
- Open your eyes, stretch your arms over the top of your head, and say, "Yes!"
- Notice your new number on the scale (remember 0 = zero stress, the most relaxed you can be) and congratulate yourself on how quickly you improved your state!

Here is a simple summary for the process in case you need to peek your eyes open at any point for a quick reminder:

- Notice starting stress level from 0 to 10.
- Take 4 deep, slow breaths.
- Grow roots.
- Notice your palms.
- Count down from 10 to 1 saying, "I am going deeper and deeper" after each number.
- Repeat the hypno-affirmations "I am grateful for _____ (choose a person). I am grateful for _____ (choose a place). I am grateful for _____ (choose a body part)" 10 times.
- Imagine being filled with gratitude for the rest of the day.
- Smile while opening your eyes and say, "Yes!"
- Notice new number on the scale of 0 to 10.
- Congratulate yourself for improving your state so quickly!

In this self-hypnosis script we added one new step, which is to bring our focus and awareness and attention to the palm of our hands. Let's discuss why:

**Why do we bring our attention to the palm of our hands?**
This is a wonderful technique I learned from reading Eckhart Tolle's books. Bringing your focus and awareness and attention to the sensations in your palms is one of the fastest ways to return to the present moment. The present moment is the only time where lasting transformation can take place (as it is the only time that actually exists!) and so this step helps to bring us back from worrying about the past or obsessing about the future into the one moment where we can actually improve our lives, right now.

# Next Steps

Excellent! You have completed the Infinite Gratitude self-hypnosis process!

- Now, go ahead and visit www.CloseYourEyesGetFree .com to access this chapter's hypnosis recording. Pop in your headphones, sit back, relax, and Close Your Eyes, Get Free.
- After you listen to the recording, please let me know how it went! Using the hashtag #CloseYourEyesGetFree on Instagram or Twitter, message me @GraceSmithTV your starting and ending numbers on the stress scale. By using the hashtag, you'll get to see how other readers

are improving right alongside you, plus I will have an opportunity to cheer you on!

- Move on to Chapter 4 and look out for all of the wonderful benefits you're already starting to receive as a result of learning the power of hypnosis.

# Chapter 4

# The Science of Hypnosis

Linda sat looking at her computer screen for a long time. Her heart was already racing. She had just received an e-mail that contained the opportunity of a lifetime; to present to the entire board of directors the project she had been overseeing for the past year. She knew her numbers, her projections had been conservative, and she was over performing. Everything was on track, and she knew the board would be thrilled. They would absolutely roll her program out company-wide now that she had proven her strategy was such a success regionally. There was only one problem. She was now based out of the Chicago office and this year the board's retreat would be held in their newest offices; not New York, not Los Angeles, not in Miami, not even in London.

Linda's mouth was already beginning to feel dry, it was difficult to swallow, and her hands were beginning to shake involuntarily.

This year the board retreat would be held in . . . Hong Kong.

Ever since the tragedy of 9/11, Linda's fear of flying was debilitating. Whenever possible she would drive to or even take trains to US-based meetings. The few hellish times when she had to travel by plane to London, she knocked herself out with a Xanax and a few too many drinks. She would feel awful for at least two days between the hangover and the jet lag, yet she could muster the trip.

Hong Kong, though? There was just no way. She would have to cancel, or worse yet, let someone unqualified take the credit for her career-defining project. Sure, they would say her name a half-dozen times throughout the presentation, but the glory always goes to the one presenting.

She snapped closed her laptop and grabbed her coat; she needed some fresh air.

Once she was outside, the biting cold of Chicago's winter winds sliced right through her many layers. Her cheeks turned an immediate three shades brighter and her hands dug down deeper into her pockets. She had moved to Chicago in 2002, when she realized she just wasn't moving past that horrific day in New York and it wasn't looking as if she ever would. Linda used to be based in the downtown NYC office, so close to the Twin Towers that she still couldn't walk on Wall Street without seeing it covered in a film of dust. She had lost so many friends, and her friends had lost so many friends. The pain was unbearable and the memories just wouldn't fade.

Prior to 2001, Linda still hadn't *loved* flying but she didn't hate it. Her mother had always been pretty nervous on family vacations, taking deep breaths, tightening the seatbelt until she could barely breathe, watching the fly attendants like a hawk as they went through the motions of what to do during an emergency landing. Linda grew up watching her mother fly this way and she just adopted some of the same habits and fears. But once they were in the air, she and her mother would calm down; it was really only during taxi, take-off, and landing that they used to have a rough time.

After 9/11, though, Linda was inconsolable. She already needed more than two hands to count the number of times she walked halfway down the "gangplank" as she would call it, before turning around, running back up toward the airport to tell the agent at the desk still scanning tickets "I just can't do it; give mine to someone on standby," and forfeiting hundreds of dollars on a flight she would need to later rebook so as to not lose her job.

She was already on thin ice. Linda had essentially been promoted as many times as someone could be promoted before her job required more travel. She had turned down three growth opportunities within the company, citing her PTSD, and her boss, although sympathetic, was also on edge: during the last quarterly review, in no uncertain terms she had told Linda she couldn't continue to make more money for doing the same job forever, even though her expertise and deliverables were more and more impressive. Essentially, Linda would either need to learn to be okay with regular international travel, or she would need to move on to another job.

This trip to Hong Kong felt like a test. It would catapult her to new levels within the company, or it would be the kiss of death.

Linda ducked inside a Starbucks to get out of the cold and called her best friend. Over a piping hot latte she filled Mikaela in, finishing with, "I guess this is it. I'll have to start all over. No one will hire me at this same level unless I'm okay to travel. From here on out, I either need to start over or be okay with going backward."

Mikaela replied, "The thing I always find so amazing is that it terrifies you to get to the meetings, but once you're there, you shine. You love public speaking! Whereas I always get so nervous speaking in front of *anyone*; whether it's ten people I know or a hundred strangers, I'm equally shaking like a leaf. You know, my

HR department is now offering this group hypnotherapy class once a week to overcome fear of public speaking. I haven't tried it yet but a few colleagues are already swearing by it. I wonder if the same hypnotherapist could help you with your fear of flying."

Linda was at her wits' end and was willing to try anything. Mikaela quickly looked up the contact information for the hypnotherapist inside her company's directory and within thirty minutes Linda had booked her first appointment.

A week later, Linda and Mikaela met for dinner. "So, how did it go with the hypnotherapy? Are you cured?" Mikaela asked.

"Well, I don't know about 'cured' just yet," Linda said with a smile, "But it was really interesting, actually. The hypnotherapist said that while many fears or phobias can be almost entirely irrational, which actually makes them even easier to overcome, the fear of flying is at least partially legitimate. Even though it is technically much safer to fly than it is to drive in terms of the likelihood of ending up in accident; of course, not all car accidents are fatal and with plane crashes . . . well, you get the point. So, basically I had to thank my subconscious for trying to keep me safe, to let it know that I appreciated its concern, but ultimately the fear of flying was hurting me a lot more than flying itself ever had. We had to focus on tangible data in my life, essentially that the *fear* of flying has caused real, true damage in my life, whereas with flying itself I have always arrived perfectly safe and sound wherever I was going. This logic while in hypnosis seemed to create some kind of shift and I really felt it. We then visualized my easily staying calm on the plane and the hypnotherapist made me a recording I can listen to during takeoff and landing. I mean, I guess I won't know if it really worked until the next time I'm boarding a plane, but I have to say, when I think about flying I'm not having the same racing heart or shaking hands or terrible thoughts. I just feel slightly apprehensive, as I used to when I was younger. I'm going back for a follow-up session next week and the flight to Hong Kong is a week after that, so I'll have a few more days to decide whether my career is going to sink or swim." Mikaela lifted her glass and clinked Linda's: "Here's hoping hypnosis works."

A year later, Mikaela and Linda met up at their favorite nail salon for a pedicure. As soon as they settled down in their comfy chairs and the treatment began, Mikaela reached down and pulled a little present out of her purse. She handed the bright little package to Linda, saying, "Congratulations to the most fabulous global manager I've ever laid eyes on—I'm so proud of you!"

..................................................

This story is derived from a real client I had who was truly on the brink of losing her job, only to turn her fear of flying around so thoroughly that within a year she was promoted to global manager. The power of the mind is truly astounding. Did you know that Thomas Edison and Albert Einstein used hypnosis? There are actually many innovators, creative visionaries, and top athletes who use hypnosis to access the theta brain wave state to enhance their performance. James Earl Jones, the voice of Darth Vader, used hypnosis to overcome stuttering, Tiger Woods has used it to improve his golf game, the late Princess Diana used it to overcome her fear of public speaking, Ben Affleck (and too many other celebrities to list) used it to quit smoking, and many Olympic athletes use it to prepare for competition.

Thomas Edison is well known for his "naps," which were actually a deeply relaxed state between waking consciousness and sleep, where creativity flowed like a child's. In this state, he was delightfully uninhibited and unencumbered by self-criticism. Edison would put himself into a hypnotic state while holding a metal ball in his hand. If he relaxed deeper than he had intended, moving from theta to delta (sleep), the metal ball would drop into a metal pan beneath his hand, waking him so that he could start again. Accessing this state allowed him to problem-solve on a subconscious level where "ah-ha" moments necessary for breakthroughs often occur.

Scientific and clinical studies at the Mayo Clinic, Yale University, and Stanford University continue to shed scientific light on the efficacy of hypnosis, and in preparation for this book I was lucky enough to work with Dr. Keerthy Sunder and Samantha Franklin of Mind and Body Treatment and Research Institute in Southern California on our own study. You'll find more info about our study in just a few pages, but let me take a few moments to introduce Dr. Sunder and Samantha, as I will be referencing their insights quite a bit throughout this chapter.

We met a conference in Denver, Colorado, and instantly, Dr. Sunder, Samantha, and I knew that we had shared missions and interests. We stayed in touch, and a few months later, my husband and I had the pleasure of visiting Dr. Sunder and Samantha at their institute in California. We had planned for a two-hour visit but ended up staying for fourteen hours. We learned all about the fascinating use of neurofeedback and TMS (transcranial magnetic stimulation), which are offered at the institute, and I was thrilled to answer all of their questions as they were deeply interested in hypnotherapy and how it could be used as an adjunct tool to help their patients.

We then decided to conduct an informal study specifically for this book (found at the end of this chapter and in the appendix) to measure outcomes of one week of hypnotherapy. One week may seem like a short time, but even one session of hypnosis has often proved to be extraordinarily life-altering. So, while short and sweet, the information garnered from this study is as telling as it is fascinating.

Keerthy Sunder, the medical director and founder of Mind and Body Treatment and Research Institute, has more than twenty years of experience as a medical doctor and holds diplomas from the American Board of Psychiatry and Neurology, American Board of Addiction Medicine, and the Royal College of Obstetricians and Gynecologists, London. His membership list in the field of mental health and addiction is extensive and includes a Distinguished Fellow of the American Psychiatric Association. He also serves as a board member of the National Alliance on Mental Illness (NAMI), San Jacinto, and an editorial board member for the *Journal of Addiction Therapy and Research*, to name a few. He is a Dream Builder member of the Academy of Integrative Health and Medicine (AIHM), a member of the credentialing committee for the American Board of Addiction Medicine, and an accredited menopause practitioner. He speaks internationally, has had numerous professional articles published, and is author of the best-selling *Addictions: Face Your Addiction and Save Your Life*. His passion is to integrate the mind, body, and soul in medicine. In addition to all of this, he is an incredibly kind, welcoming, and genuine man.

Samantha Franklin is a neuromodulation technologist who is also the practice director for the Mind and Body Treatment and Research Institute. Her background is in biomedical study at the University of California, Riverside, and she is a strong proponent of therapeutic modalities, such as hypnosis, mindfulness meditation, neurofeedback, and TMS. (Samantha is also a world-class musician who played stand-in bass for albums recorded at Abbey Road Studios in London. Whereas my all-girl rock band from yesteryear came to an end after a few short months, Samantha's played the Warped Tour. We're two ladies who are equally as passionate about making the world a better place through accessing the subconscious mind as we are about music. It was the bedrock for endless geeking out.)

In short, working with Dr. Sunder and Samantha Franklin has been a dream come true. Often, it's difficult to ascertain the true impact of hypnotherapy because there are so many variables, as every hypnotherapist uses different words and a different approach in his or her practice, and each has different levels of rapport with clients. Furthermore, all clients come to the session with different expectations, which can significantly impact how they might respond to various suggestions. With that in mind, I set out to conduct my own study for the purposes of this book, and I was lucky enough to have the immense support and knowledge of Dr. Sunder and Samantha.

Although the power of hypnosis has been evidenced in client testimonials and in the fact that the world's elite have been using this tool for centuries, the science behind it is now finally catching up. Let's review some of what we now know about this tool, which has been mired in mystery and misunderstanding for far too long, beginning with the findings of our study.

# Our Study: The Power of Hypnosis

Over one hundred people started the study, and thirty-five completed it from beginning to end. We used only data from those who completed the study. This shows us that the first hurdle to overcome is showing up for our daily commitments. Hypnosis only works if we actually do it! (To help with this, I've created a hypnosis recording to help increase your desire and commitment to actually complete your hypnosis every day. You can find it at www.CloseYourEyesGetFree.com. For more information, see page 259.)

The study included listening to the same hypnosis recording once per day for seven days in a row and completing a quiz before and after. We measured twenty-one positive emotions and forty negative ones, as well as overall stress levels. We chose these emotions based on words commonly used during therapy sessions and on intake forms. (For the full list, see the Appendix.) The answers were randomized so that every time the quiz was taken, the answers were in a different order.

The biggest increases showed that on average participants were 32 percent happier, 29 percent more content, and 27 percent more satisfied after seven days of listening to the hypnosis recording. Decreases in emotion were even more significant, which is interesting. This suggests that it is faster to let go of a habit than to create one. At the same time, participants felt on average 80 percent less disdain; 80 percent, less furious and disgusted; 58.8 percent, less depressed; and 54.5 percent, less angry, and the feeling of procrastination decreased by 51.5 percent. In addition, although stress levels decreased dramatically immediately following the recording, stress levels were still lower than ever by the end of the week. How much did overall stress levels decrease? By 45.5 percent.

How would you like to be 45.5 percent less stressed out, 32 percent happier, and 51.5 percent less likely to procrastinate in just seven days? Amazing, isn't it?

For a greater in-depth understanding of our study, please turn to page 255 of the Appendix.

Now that we've reviewed the basic findings of our study, let's dive deeper into the science behind how and why hypnosis works. I asked Dr. Sunder and Samantha to provide us with some answers to help us further understand how hypnosis works within the framework of our complicated mind:

**Q:** What is the mind?

**A:** The mind is the home for consciousness. It represents the software that allows for the manifestation of thought, memory, and imagination.

**Q:** What is the subconscious mind?

**A:** It is the part of the mind that we cannot access readily but stores our emotions, feelings, and memories. It's also the receptacle for our imagination, intuition, and spiritual experiences.

**Q:** What is the brain?

**A:** The brain is the physical home where the mind resides.

**Q:** What are brain waves?

**A:** Brain waves are the building blocks of our consciousness. They facilitate a complex system of communication and operate like a symphony orchestrated by the brain cells or neurons.

**Q:** How do we measure brain waves?

**A:** Delicate sensors are applied to the surface of the scalp that capture the electrical activity of the brain waves. The four brain waves of delta, theta, alpha, and beta are characterized by unique bandwidth frequencies and reflect states of consciousness ranging from alertness to deep sleep.

**Q:** What is the mind-body connection?

**A:** States of dysregulation have their origins in the disruption of mind/body barriers. The psyche (the human soul, mind, or spirit) and the soma (the body as distinct from the soul, mind, or psyche) are inextricably connected.

**Q:** What are neurons?

**A:** Neurons are the foundational building blocks of the nervous system. They are the conduits of electrical and chemical communication.

**Q:** What does it mean when we say, "Neurons that fire together, wire together"?

**A:** The brain is an adaptive and plastic organ. When we pay attention to happy thoughts and experiences, the nerve cells fire and wire in the direction of promoting blissful states. The opposite is also true. When we repeatedly pay attention to sad thoughts and feelings, the nerve cells fire and hardwire negative patterns. This phenomenon is also referred to as neuroplasticity.

**Q:** What is the "reptilian brain"?

**A:** It's the oldest part of the evolutionary brain that is responsive to our primal desire to survive by flight or fight. It's an unregulated response expressed by the part of the brain also called the limbic brain.

**Q:** Without having formally studied hypnotherapy, but knowing all you do about how the brain functions, what are your thoughts on how hypnotherapy works?

**A:** Hypnosis is a process that produces this increased awareness of the unconscious mind, heightened sense of suggestibility, and deep relaxation to access the subconscious mind without resistance. This allows for brain wave state shifts to take place to promote wellness and recovery.

**Q:** In the same way, without having formally studied hypnotherapy, what are your thoughts on why hypnotherapy is so effective?

**A:** Hypnotherapy does not access willpower but has the amazing ability to utilize the power of imagination and effect a change in reality by accessing the subconscious mind.

**Q:** What is neurofeedback?

**A:** Neurofeedback is a noninvasive, nonpharmaceutical brain exercise. We show your brain a reflection of its own activity while you sit back and enjoy a movie or a video game driven by your own brain waves. This allows your brain to recalibrate and self-regulate its own functionality over time. Neurofeedback trains your brain to self-regulate, much like a workout for the mind. This self-regulation helps your brain flex its own muscle using neuroplasticity. Self-regulation training strengthens and enhances the overall function of the central nervous system, thereby ramping up and improving mental performance, emotional control, and physiological stability.

**Q:** What are your thoughts on other factors impacting the brain?

**A:** The timeless pursuit of tranquility and inner peace has inspired a remarkably effective heuristic of [examining of] wellness practices. Ancient holistic healing and rejuvenation techniques allow us to broaden the focus from simply treating specific maladies or conditions to embracing patients as whole beings so as to achieve optimal health. A voluminous amount of scientific research currently validates the untapped power and efficacy of holistic patient care. Mindfulness meditation, yoga, acupuncture, hypnotherapy, therapeutic massage, and optimal brain-healthy nutrition are integral to gaining a proper balance in life.

Now that Dr. Sunder and Samantha have provided us with a general understanding of the mind, let's dive even deeper into the science.

# Brain Waves

I think it's safe to say we all know the brain is infinitely complex. To explain how the brain functions in any detail is quite the undertaking, but there are a few main areas that are helpful to understand before we continue on our hypnotic adventure. Furthermore, in my professional opinion, learning the science behind hypnosis allows the common misconceptions about it to finally be put to rest, and more important, the invaluable efficacy of hypnotherapy to be finally understood in a practical sense.

Let's start with brain waves. We've discussed brain waves a lot already, especially the "theta brain wave state" that you enter into during hypnosis. But what is a brain wave exactly, and how is it measured? Put simply, brain waves are synchronized electrical pulses between neurons that are communicating messages.

Have you ever seen a movie where a patient has sensors placed on his or her scalp, and there are wires from the sensors to machines? Those brain waves are being measured in hertz (cycles per second). In general, brain waves can range from slow and subtle to fast and complex. If your brain waves measure as slow, you may be feeling tired or sluggish. If they measure high, you may be feeling "wired" and alert. Brain waves are a continued stream of consciousness that range in variation depending on what you're doing or feeling.

There are six brain wave levels: infra-low, delta, theta, alpha, beta, and gamma. When it comes to hypnosis, theta brain waves are the doorway to memory and learning. Vivid imagery, strong intuition, and information from your unconscious become available to you while your mind is in this state. It's the state we are all in as soon as we wake up in the morning and right before we fall asleep at night. Have you ever awakened and felt as if you were still in your dream and could remember it perfectly? Then, as you woke up even more, did the dream seem to slip away? This is the transition from a theta brain wave state up through alpha and into the waking state of beta. Hypnosis takes place anywhere from light alpha to deep delta. However, it's most associated with the theta brain wave range, which is a wonderfully deep meditative state that allows our mind to uncover stored memories. Our problem-solving abilities increase, as does our overall creativity. In the theta brain wave state, we tend to feel safe and relaxed, which also allows us to become highly suggestible to suggestions that are in line with our personal goals for transformation.

In general, if your perception changes, then your brain waves change. Medication and recreational drugs alter brain waves. Meditation and yoga, along with neurofeedback, transcranial magnetic stimulation (see page 95 for more on this), and, of course, hypnotherapy can train brain waves to be calm and peaceful. The more we practice these modalities, the more balanced the mind becomes.

## Neurons

Early on in my private practice, I began using visualizations with my clients. After Alexandre's initial success with this technique, I would have them imagine their brain like an aerial photo of a city at night, thinking of certain parts of the brain as having a blackout, meaning they were completely dark with no sign of life or electricity. They would describe the parts of their brain that were hustling and bustling with bright lights and tons of electricity, and they would describe what each area of the brain represented to them. Once they identified the area that was their issue, we would rework the system. If the anxiety part of their brain was extremely bright and over-working, and it looked like a system-overload, we would turn off some of those lights until it calmed down. This freed-up additional energy to work on another area. For example, if there was a lack of motivation, we would add electricity to the motivation part of the brain, turning on the lights there. This worked extremely well. When I spoke with Dr. Keerthy about the phenomenon, he said it's likely that the neurons were being mentally redirected in the brain.

Neurons are equally as important to understand as brain waves, as both are cornerstones of how hypnosis functions in our mind. Our brain is basically a mass of interconnected neurons, constantly communicating with one another. More specifically, "cells within the nervous system, called neurons, communicate with each other in unique ways. The neuron is the basic working unit of the brain, a specialized cell designed to transmit information to other nerve cells, muscle or gland cells."[1]

There are now conflicting reports on how many neurons are in the human brain; however, for some time, most neuroscientists have estimated that there are approximately 100 billion neurons in the brain. 100 billion! Neurons send and receive messages via an electrical impulse that can be measured as our brain waves. The neurons and brain waves work together to create memories, influence how we feel, and influence what we think about.

To help explain how this works within the context of hypno-therapy, I'll use the analogy of a highway. Every time you think a thought, feel an emotion, or take an action, it is as if a little dirt path is being carved out in your mind (a neural pathway). Over time, through repetition, that the dirt path becomes a little two-lane road; the more you repeat those thoughts, emotions, and actions, the faster that little road becomes paved; and over the years, that little dirt path can turn into a sixteen-lane highway in the brain—with countless entry ramps. For example, if nail-biting started off as a little dirt path and happened only because of one little trigger, let's say when you actually had a broken nail, but over the years you started biting your nails for countless reasons—boredom, stress, frustration, anger, and most insidious of all, habit—those become countless new entry ramps that have been built to this now sixteen-lane highway in the brain. Hypnotherapy allows us to put up orange traffic cones in front of that old highway, blocking access to it, but it only lasts if we quickly build another dirt path, a different option to cope with stress, frustration, and so on. Every hypnosis session strengthens and deepens that path so that before you know it, you have a new sixteen-lane highway in the brain, one that you created for yourself rather than one that was built by default.

## ······· NEUROFEEDBACK AND TRANSCRANIAL ······· MAGNETIC STIMULATION

When I first began working with Dr. Keerthy Sunder and Samantha Franklin, I was shocked to learn about two new breakthroughs in technology that are tremendously effective in combating depression and anxiety with little to no side effects—neurofeedback and transcranial magnetic stimulation (TMS). As soon as I learned about them, I felt the way I did when Alexandre broke through his paralysis—that everyone needs to know about it! Here is a brief primer on these fantastic new tools.

Neurofeedback can be thought of as a brain exercise. It checks the condition of your mind's brain waves and retrains them with its own feedback. It's a computer-assisted therapy whereby sensors are attached to the scalp and an analysis of your brain activity is conducted. A reflection of the brain's own activity is then reflected back, which recalibrates and self-regulates its function over time. It targets the bioelectrical functioning of the brain and attempts to improve psychological stability, mental performance, and emotional control over time.[2] It helps with a variety of issues, such as drug and alcohol abuse, depression, attention deficits, and stress relief. It can even boost an individual's abilities when it comes to sports, arts, and business.

> TMS uses energy generated by pulsed magnetic fields to activate specific cortical neurons, as well as neural structures and pathways deep in the mid-brain that control mood and depression. The treatment entails applying a device with a magnetic coil to the head over the left prefrontal cortex area. Throughout the treatment, the TMS system delivers enough stimulation in the predetermined area to get the designated neurons to activate and release the necessary chemical messengers that help to relieve the symptoms of depression. These activated neurons then stimulate deeper brain regions via known proximal pathways in an almost "domino effect." This series of events happens upwards of 3,000 to 5,000 times per treatment session. Over the course of the average treatment, the brain practices these positive activation patterns so many times that it becomes able to do this on its own once treatment is completed.[3]

Both neurofeedback and TMS are noninvasive and nonpharmaceutical treatments, and they're thought of as cutting-edge treatments to relieve various mental issues. They can also be thought of as alternative therapies, such as hypnotherapy. However, the science behind these modalities are factual, and the growing success is evident.

...........................................................................................

## The Tortoise, the Dolphin, and the Hare

One of the most interesting things I learned while working with Dr. Sunder and Samantha was that they never treat their patients for things like improving peak performance until such issues as depression and anxiety have been cleared up. I realized that without having made a conscious decision, my own sessions had always been structured the same way. Until trauma and pervasive negativity are healed, it's nearly impossible to see a breakthrough in something like attracting love into one's life.

We have three primary sections of the brain. One is ancient, primitive, and keeps us alive. The second is in charge of our emotions, and the third is the most sophisticated and the most recent. They are the reptilian brain, the limbic brain, and the neocortex brain, respectively. Because I remember all things that have to do with animals, I refer to them in my mind as the Tortoise, the Dolphin, and the Hare. Essentially, we have to first work on improving the ancient tortoise before we can work with the emotional dolphin, and finally, we can catch up with the rapidly moving hare.

These three parts of the brain have evolved over millions of years and are known as today's brain, which, by the way, is still evolving. Take a look at this chart from thebrain.mcgill.ca:

| The **reptilian brain**, the oldest of the three, controls the body's vital functions such as heart rate, breathing, body temperature, and balance. Our reptilian brain includes the main structures found in a reptile's brain: the brainstem and the cerebellum. The reptilian brain is reliable but tends to be somewhat rigid and compulsive. | The **limbic brain** emerged in the first mammals. It can record memories of behaviours that produced agreeable and disagreeable experiences, so it is responsible for what are called emotions in human beings. The main structures of the limbic brain are the hippocampus, the amygdala, and the hypothalamus. The limbic brain is the seat of the value judgments that we make, often unconsciously, that exert such a strong influence on our behaviour. | The **neocortex** first assumed importance in primates and culminated in the human brain with its two large cerebral hemispheres that play such a dominant role. These hemispheres have been responsible for the development of human language, abstract thought, imagination, and consciousness. The neocortex is flexible and has almost infinite learning abilities. The neocortex is also what has enabled human cultures to develop. |
| --- | --- | --- |

These three parts of the brain do not operate independently of one another. They have established numerous interconnections through which they influence one another. The neural pathways from the limbic system to the cortex, for example, are especially well developed."[4]

Here's an interesting exercise: Write down all of the areas of your life that you would like to improve. Then, put them into a category based on which brain they're associated with. You'll have a blueprint for exactly the areas you want to work on first, second, and third as you move from the most primitive part of the brain, through the emotional brain, and finally into the "peak performance" brain.

| Reptilian—<br>work on these first: | Limbic—<br>work on these second: | Neocortex—<br>work on these areas last: |
|---|---|---|
| instincts<br>breathing<br>digestion<br>circulation<br>elimination<br>temperature<br>fight<br>flight<br>movement<br>posture | anger<br>sadness<br>disappointment<br>fear<br>anxiety | make smarter decisions<br>more focus/less distraction<br>plan for future success<br>strengthen willpower<br>learn a new language |

| Reptilian | Limbic | Neocortex |
|---|---|---|
| Stress relief* | Stress relief* | Increase self-worth |
| Overcome anxiety* | Overcome anxiety* | Stop negative thinking and complaints |
| Overcome fear of flying | Overcome depression | Breakthrough procrastination |
| | Increasing comfort/decrease pain | Weight loss/stop overeating |
| | Stop nail-biting | Quit smoking |
| | Develop gratitude | Increase self-confidence |
| | Increase self-love | Anger management |
| | Overcome insomnia | Improve relationships |
| | Increase patience and kindness | Learn a new language |
| | | Increase motivation |

* Stress relief and overcome anxiety are found in both the reptilian and limbic areas of the brain.

# What Does the Medical Community Have to Say About Hypnosis?

Some of my all-time favorite studies about hypnosis include the following takeaways:

- A study by Alfred A. Barrios, PhD, conducted in Los Angeles in 1970 and first printed in *Psychotherapy: Theory, Research and Practice*, compared recovery rates for various modalities of therapy and found the following:

  - 600 sessions of psychoanalysis have an average recovery rate of 38%.
  - 22 sessions of behavioral therapy have an average recovery rate of 72%.
  - 6 sessions of hypnotherapy have an average recovery rate of 93%.[5]
  - 6 sessions resulting in 93% improvement!

  Can you believe this information has been known for over 46 years and still hypnosis has yet to be covered by insurance companies?

- The effect of psychosocial intervention on time of survival of 86 patients with metastatic breast cancer was studied prospectively. The 1-year intervention consisted of weekly supportive group therapy with self-hypnosis for pain. Women with metastatic breast cancer who received group hypnosis therapy were able to reduce their pain experience by 50% compared to a control group.[6] At a 10-year follow-up of these same women, the hypnosis treatment group had double the survival rate of the control group.[7]

- Studies from Harvard Medical School show that hypnosis significantly reduces the time it takes to heal. Six weeks after an ankle fracture, those in the hypnosis group showed the equivalent of 8½ weeks of healing.[8]
- Out of 1,000 irritable bowel syndrome (IBS) patients treated with 12 sessions of hypnotherapy, 76% of the patients improved from the treatment. Success rates were higher for females than males (80% vs. 62%) and slightly higher in patients with anxiety (79% vs. 71%). In addition to bowel symptom improvement, nongastrointestinal symptoms also improved significantly on average after treatment, and hypnotherapy also improved the quality of life scores.[9]

Throughout this book we will discuss many ways in which hypnosis can be used to make us feel better—for example, to expedite the healing of bones, to treat IBS, or to calm nausea during chemotherapy treatments—as well as other ways in which it can expedite healing. For this chapter's self-hypnosis process I have included a script that will help bring ease and comfort to any area of your body that is experiencing pain or discomfort. This is not meant to be used in lieu of anesthesia during a surgery, as that requires extensive conditioning and an on-site certified hypnotherapist; however, for general aches, pains, and headaches, this process will be a wonderful remedy.

## Self-Hypnosis Process: Increasing Comfort/Decreasing Pain

I suggest reading through the following directions two or three times before beginning so that you will be able to follow along easily. Remember, there are video tutorials and audio recordings available to you at www.CloseYourEyesGetFree.com that will help you to become a self-hypnosis pro in no time at all.

- Begin by making note of your starting stress level. 10 = a full-blown panic attack and 0 = zero stress, no stress at all, the most relaxed a person can possibly be. Remember this number.
- Sit in a comfortable chair and place your feet flat on the ground, rest your hands gently in your lap.
- With your spine straight but comfortable, take 4 deep, slow breaths, inhaling through the nose for 4 counts and exhaling out the nose for 8 counts.
- Close your eyes and imagine gentle roots growing from the bottom of your feet down into the center of the Earth, grounding you.
- Imagine a color you love flowing in through the top of your head, all the way through your body, out the bottoms of your feet and down those roots, down into the center of the Earth.
- Bring all of your focus and awareness and attention to the palms of your hands. Perhaps you can feel your palms tingling, perhaps you can feel your heartbeat in your hands, perhaps you notice a sensation of expansion in your hands. Just notice and breathe for a few moments (you can choose whatever length of time feels best, about 30 seconds is my personal favorite).
- With your eyes closed, count down from 10 to 1, saying "I am going deeper and deeper" after each number: Ten, I am going deeper and deeper. Nine, I am going deeper

and deeper. Eight, I am going deeper and deeper. Seven, I am going deeper and deeper. Six, I am going deeper and deeper. Five, I am going deeper and deeper. Four, I am going deeper and deeper. Three, I am going deeper and deeper. Two, I am going deeper and deeper. One, I am going deeper and deeper...

- With your eyes closed, repeat the following hypno-affirmations silently in your mind or out loud, 10 times: I send my _____ [body part] love and relaxation. I feel myself improving. I am safe.
- Take another nice, deep, letting-go breath and with your eyes closed imagine all of the pain draining away from that part of the body. Pretend that loving, calm, healing energy is now soothing that part of your body. See, feel, and experience comfortable relief all over.
- Once you've spent 1–2 minutes imagining that part of your body healing and becoming comfortable, imagine the same color as before flowing in through the top of your head, all the way through your body, out the bottoms of your feet, and down those roots into the center of the Earth.
- Put a gentle smile on your lips, open your eyes, stretch your arms over the top of your head, and say, "Yes!"
- Notice your new number on the scale (remember 0 = zero stress, the most relaxed you can be) and congratulate yourself on how quickly you improved your state!

Here is a simple summary for the process in case you need to peek your eyes open at any point for a quick reminder:

- Notice starting stress level from 0 to 10.
- Take 4 deep, slow breaths.
- Grow roots.
- Color.
- Notice your palms.
- Count down from 10 to 1 saying, "I am going deeper and deeper" after each number.
- Repeat the hypno-affirmations, "I send my _____ [body part] love and relaxation. I feel myself improving. I am safe" 10 times.
- Imagine healing that part of your body.
- Color.
- Smile while opening your eyes and say "Yes!"
- Notice new number on the scale of 0 to 10.
- Congratulate yourself for improving your state so quickly!

In this slightly more advanced self-hypnosis script, we've added one new component, a color we love flowing through our body.

### Why do we imagine a color we love flowing in through the top of our head, all the way through our body?

Oftentimes, when we love a color, it is prominently featured throughout our wardrobe, on the walls of our home, in trinkets throughout our office, even in the jewelry and artwork that we buy. By continually running the color we love through our body, it not only calms us, it also conditions us to subconsciously feel calm every time we see that color throughout our day. You can change the color every time you practice this self-hypnosis process, or you can use the same color each time. Any color or shade will work and I tend to find that blue is the most widely used.

## Next Steps

Excellent! You have completed the Increase Comfort/Decrease Pain self-hypnosis process!

- Now, go ahead and visit www.CloseYourEyesGetFree .com to access this chapter's hypnosis recording. Pop in your headphones, sit back, relax, and Close Your Eyes, Get Free.
- After you listen to the recording, please let me know how it went! Using the hashtag #CloseYourEyesGetFree on Instagram or Twitter, message me @GraceSmithTV your starting and ending numbers on the stress scale. I'd also love to know which body part you are healing and how much comfort you were able to achieve. By using the hashtag, you'll get to see how other readers are improving right alongside you, plus I will have an opportunity to cheer you on!
- Move on to Chapter 5, and in the meantime, look out for all of the wonderful benefits you're already starting to receive as a result of learning the power of hypnosis.

Chapter 5

# The First Step to Mental Freedom: Taking Responsibility for Your Actions

Melodee was a talker. Whenever she was asked about her day, she would go on for ages, describing every little detail, every thought, every person she interacted with, and every possible outcome of every scenario. She meant well, and her friends loved her spontaneous and bubbly personality, but to get a word in edgewise during a conversation, they'd have to time it to when Melodee took a breath. At her first hypnotherapy session, her answer to "What brings you here today?" was a perfect reflection of the frenzy going on inside her mind.

"Well, my friend used hypnosis to quit smoking, so I figured I'd give it a shot because I've been in therapy for ten years. And I feel like it helped in some ways, and in other ways, I'm just getting worse. Like, I'm ten pounds heavier than I was last year, I've been single for longer than most of my friends, and I really thought I'd be further along in my career than I am now. I mean, honestly, I think I thought I'd have my boss's boss's job by now. I have some really great friends, but they're starting to get married and have babies, and even though I totally don't want or need those things right now, I definitely want them within the next three to five years. So, I guess I'm starting to panic a little because that basically means I need to meet Mr. or Ms. Right, like, right now. I just keep going on Tinder dates, and I'm always so excited about them beforehand. And afterward, I'm so depressed about the state of dating in New York City that I just eat for a bunch of hours while watching TV. There's one guy I've been out with a few times, but I'm really not sure what I'm still doing with him. Then again, the other night, he did cook me dinner, and he remembered I love quinoa with almonds and cayenne pepper. I mean, I think that's pretty specific, so if he remembered that, he must have been thinking about me. I think I always assume every guy is going to turn out like the last one, so I never give them a chance. But then, I do give them a chance, and they end up being exactly like the last one! So, I guess I shouldn't give anybody a chance! I don't know. I don't understand why this keeps happening, but if I had to guess, I would say it has something to do with my boss because I swear she just doesn't understand my potential. She doesn't understand all of the things I could bring to the company, so she never asks me for help."

At this point, the hypnotherapist gently cleared her throat. In a kind way, she said, "Melodee, thank you so much. I'm sure there's so much more you could tell me, but in the interest of time so that you can get the most out of your session, I do want to point out that hypnotherapy is quite different from regular talk therapy. We actually don't give much weight to what the conscious mind has to say or even what it thinks. This is because the conscious mind is simply a record player stuck on the same song. Your conscious words and thoughts are revealing your subconscious programming—a story that was told and retold until it became your belief system about the world you live in and your role in it. If we want to change the things we say or do or feel, we have to start seeing those undesirable thoughts, feelings, and actions as nothing more than a story. That's it—a story. If you want to change your life, you have to change the story. And if you keep telling the same story, it's like pedaling backward up a hill, totally futile because you strengthen the story every time you repeat it. So, go ahead and close your eyes, take a deep breath, and let me know in a word or two if this makes sense."

"Yes, it makes so much sense," Melodee responded. She continued at a slower pace than before. "So, every time I complained to my therapist or girlfriends about the jerk I went out with last night, instead of it relieving stress, like I thought it was, it was just making it worse?"

The hypnotherapist smiled and said, "It was strengthening the patterns of whatever was being repeated, so it sounds like it was repeating the patterns of complaining, feeling stress, feeling let down, and the expectation that all men are the same. Our expectations tend to be self-fulfilling prophecies because we make decisions that are in alignment with our worldview."

Melodee took a deep breath and looked up at the ceiling for a few moments before saying, "So, by complaining about men and my boss, I've been attracting bad relationships. It's why I keep getting passed over for a raise?"

"Maybe, maybe not. But imagine if you expected every guy you met to be genuinely kind, perhaps not perfect for you, but kind. Could that potentially change the types of people you swipe right for on Tinder? If you assumed your boss knew all of your best qualities and that she wanted what is best for you, do you think you would perform better or worse at work? Do you think it might change how you interact with her and that it might improve her view of you and your abilities?"

"Oh my god! Do you know how many brunches with bottomless mimosas and hours of bitching to my girlfriends I've had in my life? I think I may have been strengthening all of the wrong things pretty much forever."

As Melodee's eyes began to well up with tears, the hypnotherapist said, "What a wonderful thing that you've learned this now and will know the deep peace that comes from writing your own story, instead of perpetuating the one that was written for you by your parents, society, and advertising companies."

Melodee laughed and said, "Wow, if *they* wrote my story, no wonder I'm such a mess."

The hypnotherapist laughed. "You know, I wrote a book about this, and the title was almost 'Brainwash Yourself or Everyone Else Will' because it's really quite true. If we don't take the reins of our own subconscious programming, everyone else will, without our being aware of it. Now, you're going to see in just a moment that the difference between communication on the conscious level and communication on the subconscious level is fascinating. Once you enter into hypnosis, you'll become aware of a resource state where problem-solving is easy and where you can reach the core of an issue very, very quickly. So, let's choose one area of your life where, if you were to transform that, everything else would improve. What comes to mind first?"

Melodee thought about it for a moment before speaking, which was already a sign that a shift was taking place. Then, she said, "I honestly think if I didn't hate my job, where I spend most of my life, that I wouldn't put so much pressure on the dates to make me happy, and I wouldn't feel so ashamed about my friends moving on with their lives with raises or promotions or weddings or babies. And I think I'd eat less if I felt proud of my work. So, let's start with career."

"Fabulous. It's really helpful if you simply tell me in one sentence how you currently feel about your career. Then, tell me in one sentence how you *want* to feel or what habit you want to have instead."

"I feel ashamed and embarrassed. I want to feel motivated and proud."

"Great, let's begin. Close your eyes."

They both smiled as Melodee closed her eyes and took a nice, deep, letting-go breath.

........................................

## The Truth (and the Lies)

In Melodee's story, the hypnotherapist's role was to help her shift from focusing on what I would call lies, to focusing on the Truth. The Truth is singular: You are perfect. Other ways to say it include: You are worthy. You are loved. This isn't based in any religion, although many religions were initially based on the Truth.

Although we have discussed "reprogramming," "transforming," and "improving," none of this is really *true*. These terms make what we're doing easy to understand and comprehend, especially in the "self-improvement or bust" kind of world that we live in, but it doesn't make it true. The Truth is that you are already perfect. Something that's perfect can't be improved upon or fixed because there's nothing broken. The fact is that you're not actually hypnotizing yourself; you are *de*-hypnotizing yourself.

A lot of spiritual teachers talk about the stories we tell ourself. I do agree that they are stories. However, to me, stories are what I heard at bedtime. They were innocuous. What we tell ourself are *lies*. These lies are insidious, and the world suffers terribly because of them. It's a lie that we're separate from one another; it's a lie that one life is worth more than another; and it's a lie that we're too fat, thin, rich, or poor.

You are perfect. You are perfect. You are perfect. Say it with me: "I am perfect, I am perfect, I am perfect."

Take a nice, deep, letting-go breath, and repeat it again: "I am perfect, I am perfect, I am perfect." You very well may be thinking, "Seriously, Grace? After learning that my brain is firing in ways that don't serve me, you're now telling me I'm perfect?"

Yes! Everyone who has ever looked into the eyes of a baby knows that when we first show up on this planet, we are 100 percent perfect, and that essence is not erased over time, it is simply buried. Through the process of de-hypnosis, we are going to peel away all of those layers upon layers of conditioning and get back to the source, get back to who you truly are: perfect, whole, and complete.

This is why I *love* what I've learned from the Mind and Body Research Institute, which we discussed at length in Chapter 4. You *are* perfect. Through all of these years of conditioning, your brain has simply developed dark spots in certain areas, and we're going to flip the light switch back on. You are perfect. Your brain is hardwired to believe a whole bunch of lies. You're not to blame for them, but you're responsible for getting rid of them. So, you're going to scrub and wash away the layers of muck until all that's left is the core, the Truth, which is that you are perfect.

# Your Purpose

A lot of my clients come to me worried about their life's purpose. As far as interests go, it's a good one to have. Hypnotherapy can help you dig out the answer much faster once you've gotten underneath the noise of the story your conscious mind has been playing on Repeat. Imagine that you're in a jam-packed noisy motorboat, choking on exhaust fumes as you move around searching for your life's purpose. The boat is packed full with people telling you their opinion about what you should do, who you should be, what's important, what will work, what won't work, how to spend your money, and so on. That's your *conscious* mind trying to figure out your life's purpose.

Now, take a nice, deep breath, and *dive* into the cool, clean, calm waters. Dive deep down. You realize that the deeper you dive, the less noise you hear. The voices are fading. You no longer hear the noisy engine, and the exhaust fumes are gone. You dive down and ask the pure, clean quietness, "What is my purpose?" And all of sudden, a massive, gorgeous clamshell opens, and your life's purpose is inscribed inside. That's your *subconscious* mind figuring out your life's purpose.

It's likely you'll realize you already knew your life's purpose and were headed down the right trail years ago, but you allowed the voices on the boat to throw you off the scent.

You get the answer from going *inward. Deeper.* You close your eyes and get free.

Remember that you get better at hypnosis over time. If you want to free dive down to get those answers, you have to learn how to train your muscles first. If the answer isn't clear just yet, keep at it.

In the meantime, what if we just assume that your job, your life's purpose, is to be kind to everyone you meet, and do what brings you joy? What if that was it?

*Your life's purpose: Be kind to everyone you meet, and do what brings you joy.*

You'd have to be nice to the poor soul who answers the phone when you call to challenge the overdraft fee you got when your Netflix charge threw your finances into a tizzy. You'd have to be nice to the scowling people on the subway. You'd have to be nice to your mom even when she disagrees with you or tells you to clean something. Can you imagine what would happen if you were nice during all of these situations? Other people might be nice back, more often than not. Then, because of that, the next generation is raised to be that way. Eventually, if we were kind to everyone and did what brought us joy, we wouldn't need hypnosis!

I realize that until we do a lot of work on our subconscious, this can be easier said than done. However, if you're concerned about your life's purpose, I welcome you to release that tight grasp on the question, "What is my purpose?" Simply allow kindness and a pursuit of what brings you long-term joy to lead the way, and allow the more refined answer to the question to reveal itself over time.

## Deconstruction of the Habits You No Longer Want

Habits are built in this order:

Subconscious programming
Conscious thoughts
Conscious actions

Unfortunately, our level of awareness is in the exact opposite order. We are most aware of the actions we take first. We know we ate the bag of chips because the bag is there, deflated and empty, and our fingers are covered in salt, oil, and crumbs. There's evidence. We're aware of some of the thoughts we think because we "hear" some of it. But there's a lot of chatter going on endlessly in the background, as we're constantly thinking, thinking, thinking. There is less concrete evidence, so we're less aware of the thoughts we think than we are of the actions we take. We have the least awareness of our subconscious programming.

Most self-help books stop at the level of the actions we take, but that isn't enough to make lasting changes, not by a long shot. However, it's the best place to *start* because we're most aware of our actions.

The way we're going to *de*construct your habits, to *de*-hypnotize you, is by moving from the greatest level of awareness to the least level of awareness. This is how you'll be able to stay the most engaged. By tracking your success, you'll remain motivated to continue.

The first action you notice has improved, the more excited you will become to take the trash out of your mind. We're going to start with what you can *see* simply because social proof is a powerful mechanism to keep going, but we're very quickly going to get to the *root issue*.

Reading self-help books and *not* improving can actually harm us. It can strengthen our sense of failure and weaken our resolve. Knowing more and more about our problems, but never learning how to change the root of the issue is not self-help; it's a setup for disappointment. Do you know someone who read *The Secret* but, instead of manifesting their dreams, became even more anxious? Suddenly, they're hyperaware of their negative thoughts, but they have no tools for diminishing them.

If bad habits are weeds, then knowledge is like throwing seeds on top of weeds. With hypnosis, we remove the weeds first and then plant the seeds in the newly cleaned-up fertile ground of the subconscious mind.

## Actions

Remember that we discussed how your habits were primarily formed through the three E's: Environment, Elders, and Entertainment? In this chapter, we begin to get our hands dirty with unraveling this conditioning. If you're anything like me or the thousands of clients I've worked with, there's at least one habit in your life that drives you crazy. Maybe you've read two or three books on the subject, attended workshops, or worked with coaches or a psychiatrist to overcome the habit. Yet it still exists in your life.

Maybe it's negative thinking, overeating, smoking, or fear of flying. Whatever it is, I suspect there's something in your life that you're desperate to overcome.

Maybe you have already reached a level of excellence and peak performance, but you've seemed to plateau. There's a pattern there, a habit that's keeping you from excelling to that next level. This process will help you with that, too.

So, when you wake up in the morning, if you're not thinking to yourself, "I'm free. Every day, I'm creating the life of my dreams. It's so good to be awake," then something could be better. Life is way too short to wake up feeling dread and regret. As if you haven't accomplished your goals, and that time is going by too quickly. "I thought I'd be so much further than I am by this age," is something I hear often from new clients.

Do you remember my invitation to you in Chapter 1? I shared with you that, in fact, you *do* have the ability to wake up and feel proud of yourself, to feel excited about the day ahead. To wake up and not be consumed by anxiety, but to feel joy and excitement. To achieve this, we need a breakthrough, and the first step to this mental freedom is going to be that breakthrough. But you have to actually follow the steps. It's actually simple. All you need is focus and commitment. So, make a commitment to read the rest of this book, and you'll continue to experience a profound shift.

I used the following four steps to mental freedom to overcome habits that were keeping me from living my best life. I've also taught these four steps to all of my individual clients, and they had the same profound, lasting results. That's what I want for you!

The first step is taking responsibility for your actions. In the following chapters, we'll cover the remaining three steps, which are: (2) taking responsibility for your thoughts, (3) reprogramming (transforming) your subconscious, and (4) giving back to others.

When we take responsibility for our actions, we claim a stake in power. When we blame others, we give our power away. If you say, "I had a terrible day because my colleague did this or that," you're giving away power to your colleague. You have put that person on a pedestal, making him or her a major player in your life. Why? Because you've given this individual the power to dictate how you feel.

When you put yourself in the position of the victim, there's a subconscious belief that one of two things is happening. *What the subconscious believes it is gaining by blaming others:*

- You're going to receive sympathy, and/or
- You're going to be excused for bad behavior.

Maybe people will feel bad for you because so many terrible things are happening in your life, or it will excuse drinking more than you should, eating more than you should, or not getting work done.

The Truth is that receiving sympathy from others and hoping to have your bad behavior excused does not help you in any way. It only harms you because it robs you of your own power. The only harm that's done is to you. In essence, by playing the victim, you victimize yourself. Now, this doesn't necessarily mean it's your fault. It doesn't mean you're meant to accept blame for everything that happens in your life. But allowing others to affect the way you feel is your responsibility.

Feel the difference in the energy between these two statements: "They did this to me" and "This happened, and this is what I'm doing about it." Read those statements again. Which one will allow you to move forward? Which will make it easier for you to live an incredible life of your own design? Which one will allow you to get free?

Now, let's go a little deeper. I've had a lot of people in my lectures and workshops ask me, "How can I take responsibility for my parents' divorce?" "How can I take responsibility for things like war and famine and terrible things that happen every day?" These are important questions.

To get the answer, let's compare the three following phrases, feeling the energy behind each:

1. "I didn't have anything to do with . . . "
2. "It's not my fault that . . . "
3. "It's my responsibility to . . . "

Read through each response below, and feel the energy behind them:

1. "I didn't have anything to do with creating this war; it's not my problem."
2. "There's a war, and it's my not my fault that it exists."
3. "There's a war, and it's my responsibility to make a positive difference in whatever way I can."

Which one of these phrases inspires action? Which one inspires excellence, living life as an example of ideals and principles, and which ones inspire lethargy, procrastination, doing less than you're capable of, or even feelings of fear?

Even if you truly believe something isn't your fault or your problem, when you feel the energy behind these phrases of shoving off responsibility and blame onto others, it's a feeling of stagnation, isn't it? It happened *to* you. You're completely out of control, so while you may be attempting to distance yourself from the situation, you're telling your subconscious and the world that you have zero power. You're claiming to be powerless.

Now, let's make this a little more practical and feel the energy behind these three phrases:

1. "My boss is a [insert appropriate expletive]."
2. "It isn't my fault that the systems at work are so convoluted, archaic, and horrible that I can't do my job."
3. "It's my job; it's my responsibility."

Only one of these phrases brings power back to you, and it's the one in which you take responsibility. How does this example carry over into the rest of your life? If you place the blame on your boss, colleagues, or the system, complaining that the meetings are too long or the clients are terrible, you're giving your power away forty hours or more every week. Then, the complaining continues about your personal life—your house is too small, your feet hurt because of your shoes, your back hurts because of the genes you got from your grandmother, and so on. Essentially, you're spending your life giving your power away.

We tend to believe we can blame everything on everyone else, but that we should still be able to find the strength within us on January 1 to begin going to the gym every day. But the truth is, you can't have both. You can't give away your power all year long and then expect to have the power it takes to form a healthy new habit overnight with sheer force of will. We weaken our resolve with every powerless thought, and then weaken it again when we can't follow through with our goals and resolutions.

What if you want to overcome a challenging habit or develop excellence somewhere in your life? You need power to be able to change, but your existing *habit* is to give your power away. The habit is to assume that everyone else has more power than you do. So, the choice is to cultivate a habit where you're powerful and in control of your life or a habit where everyone else has the power and control. Maybe your boss really is a jerk, and maybe your systems at work really are terrible. But you have a *choice* to give away your power or to become more powerful by taking responsibility for what happens in your life. It's entirely up to you.

In just a moment, I'm going to ask that you close your eyes, take a nice, deep, letting-go breath, and imagine a perfect world—a perfect utopia, the most amazing place you can possibly imagine.

You're going to imagine this for sixty seconds. Then, you'll open your eyes and continue reading. Ready? You can begin.

How do you feel after those sixty seconds? When I do this in my courses and lectures or with my individual clients, I find that almost everyone's perfect world looks nearly the same. It's fascinating. It's a place where everyone is healthy, the planet is healthy, people are nice to one another, and everyone is prosperous. Ask yourself: To create such a world, what actions would everyone in that world have to take on a daily basis, moment by moment, to make it happen? Then, more important, you have to ask yourself, "What am *I* creating?" Are your actions in alignment with what's necessary to create that perfect world where you desire to live?

When we're rude to a bank teller or a telemarketer, when we complain about how we don't have enough money, and so on, what kind of world are we creating? Are our actions manifesting the opposite of the world that we desire to live in, or are our actions manifesting a utopia? Furthermore, do we expect that other people should act in accordance with what's required to create this utopia but that we're somehow separate from this responsibility? Are we creating conflict or peace? Wealth or lack? And this means 100 percent of the time. Taking responsibility for all the good, as well as all the "bad" in our lives. I put "bad" in quotes because there really is no such thing as bad. There are only misunderstood lessons that are yet to be fully absorbed. Taking responsibility for our actions is just the first step, and when we do, we gain the power necessary to drive us through the remaining three steps to mental freedom.

As a result of taking responsibility, something wonderful happens. Procrastination ceases to be a viable option, blaming others and hoping they'll fix the world's messes also goes away. Because we're taking responsibility, there's no one to blame, and with no one to blame, there's so much less to complain about. Instead, we have room to think about how grateful we are for our incredible life.

You might be thinking, "This all sounds great, Grace, but I've been blaming for so long that my mind is riddled with negative thoughts. How do I go about changing this?"

Yes—reality check—this stuff can be challenging! You're unpacking patterns that have been around for years, perhaps for a lifetime, plus your subconscious is currently 100 percent comfy with these patterns and isn't totally stoked on the idea of change right out of the gate. At about this point in the process, a lot of my clients will say, "Grace, this is hard!" So, if you're feeling that way, you're in good company! But the truth is, it isn't *hard*. Workers who built the transcontinental railroad by hand in the 1860s had it *hard*. I like this comparison because it helps us put our perceptions back in order: building a railroad is *hard*, plugging in our headphones and closing our eyes for twenty minutes is *easy*! It just takes commitment, and that is something that our Tinder, Amazon Prime, instant gratification mind is not used to anymore. But anyone who has ever taken the time to handcraft a beautiful piece of furniture, or paint a masterpiece, or practice enough to become the best player on the team, or grow a baby for nine months, will tell you that the best things in life take time and require an investment of your energy and commitment. You can do this and you're worthy of the results. So, rather than telling yourself it is "hard," start affirming, "I am worthy of this commitment, I can put the time in, I already am."

That brings us to this chapter's self-hypnosis process, in which you'll have the opportunity to observe one area of your life where you've been blaming others and giving your power away. You'll have a chance to take responsibility and face reality. In doing so, you'll reinstate your power. Then, we'll conclude with an exercise that helps you become aware of one action step you can take today that will allow you to reclaim responsibility for the situation.

A quick note before we move on: Do I always get this 100 percent right in my own life? Am I perfect and always floating around like a Buddhist monk with a soft smile and kind eyes, never bothered by anything? Are all of my clients living like this after working with me for a handful of sessions? Through my live streaming and YouTube videos, am I creating a world full of peaceful millennial angels? Absolutely not! We're all human, and this conditioning goes deep. But I get better at it every day, and I'm 100 million times better than I used to be. Honestly, that's the only reason my life is as good as it is today. In fact, the quality of my life today is a dead-on accurate barometer of just how far I've come in implementing this first step of taking responsibility. This has been the case for all of my private clients, too. And because you're sticking with this process, it will be the case for you, too.

Blame has risen to a deafening crescendo in today's world, which means powerlessness is as an all-time high. That needs to change! I took responsibility by writing this book, and you're taking responsibility by implementing what you learn as you read. Let's do this!

## Self-Hypnosis Process: Taking Responsibility for Our Actions

I suggest reading through the following directions two or three times before beginning so that you will be able to follow along easily. Remember, there are video tutorials and audio recordings available to you at www.CloseYourEyesGetFree.com that will help you to become a self-hypnosis pro in no time at all.

- Begin by making note of your starting stress level. 10 = a full-blown panic attack and 0 = zero stress, no stress at all, the most relaxed a person can possibly be. Remember this number.

- Sit in a comfortable chair and place your feet flat on the ground, rest your hands gently in your lap.
- With your spine straight but comfortable, take 4 deep, slow breaths, inhaling through the nose for 4 counts and exhaling out the nose for 8 counts.
- Close your eyes and imagine gentle roots growing from the bottom of your feet down into the center of the Earth, grounding you.
- Imagine a color you love flowing in through the top of your head, all the way through your body, out the bottoms of your feet, and down those roots, down into the center of the Earth.
- Bring all of your focus and awareness and attention to the palms of your hands. Perhaps you can feel your palms tingling, perhaps you can feel your heartbeat in your hands, perhaps you notice a sensation of expansion in your hands. Just notice and breathe for a few moments (you can choose whatever length of time feels best, about 30 seconds is my personal favorite).
- With your eyes closed, count down from 10 to 1, saying "I am going deeper and deeper" after each number: Ten, I am going deeper and deeper. Nine, I am going deeper and deeper. Eight, I am going deeper and deeper. Seven, I am going deeper and deeper. Six, I am going deeper and deeper. Five, I am going deeper and deeper. Four, I am going deeper and deeper. Three, I am going deeper and deeper. Two, I am going deeper and deeper. One, I am going deeper and deeper . . .
- With your eyes closed, repeat the following

hypno-affirmations silently in your mind or out loud, 10 times: I take responsibility. I reclaim my power. My life is mine to create.

- Take another nice, deep, letting-go breath and with your eyes closed imagine feeling more powerful than you've ever felt. Pretend in your mind that you are replacing any negative actions with positive actions for the rest of your day until you curl up into bed tonight.
- Once you've spent 1–2 minutes imagining the rest of your day filled with feeling powerful and positive actions, imagine the same color as before flowing in through the top of your head, all the way through your body, out the bottoms of your feet, and down those roots into the center of the Earth.
- Put a gentle smile on your lips, open your eyes, stretch your arms over the top of your head, and say, "Yes!"
- Notice your new number on the scale (remember 0 = zero stress, the most relaxed you can be) and congratulate yourself on how quickly you improved your state!

Here is a simple summary of the process in case you need to peek your eyes open at any point for a quick reminder:

- Notice starting stress level from 0 to 10.
- Take 4 deep breaths.
- Grow roots.
- Color.
- Notice your palms.
- Count down from 10 to 1 saying, "I am going deeper and deeper" after each number.

- Repeat the hypno-affirmations, " I take responsibility. I reclaim my power. My life is mine to create" 10 times.
- Imagine feeling more powerful than ever while taking positive action for the rest of the day.
- Color.
- Smile while opening your eyes and say, "Yes!"
- Notice new number on the scale of 0 to 10.
- Congratulate yourself for improving your state so quickly!

# Next Steps

Excellent! You have completed one of my favorites, the Taking Responsibility self-hypnosis process!

- Now, go ahead and visit www.CloseYourEyesGetFree .com to access this chapter's hypnosis recording. Pop in your headphones, sit back, relax, and Close Your Eyes, Get Free.
- After you listen to the recording, please let me know how it went! Using the hashtag #CloseYourEyesGetFree on Instagram or Twitter, message me @GraceSmithTV your starting and ending numbers on the stress scale. By using the hashtag, you'll get to see how other readers are improving right alongside you, plus I will have an opportunity to cheer you on!
- Move on to Chapter 6 and look out for all of the wonderful benefits you're already starting to receive as a result of learning the power of hypnosis.

Chapter 6

# The Second Step: Taking Responsibility for Your Thoughts

Every morning when Susan woke up, the first thing she felt was dread, followed by panic. Her heart began to race before she even got out of bed. The kids needed to get dressed. Had they finished their homework last night? Off the top of her head, she knew she hadn't responded to two texts and three e-mails. Were the senders waiting for her response? Were they angry with her for not responding?

This particular morning, Susan knew her husband would be in a bad mood come evening if his pitch didn't go well at work, so she rolled over and said, "Good luck today."

"Great," he said in a sleepy voice. "I can't even have a moment's peace when I'm not reminded of work. Thanks a lot!" He threw the covers back and got out of bed. Then, he huffed and puffed as he brushed his teeth and washed his face.

"I can't win," she thought to herself. Suddenly, she remembered she had to return a pair of pants that didn't fit her youngest son. After getting everyone off to school and work, she headed to the office.

Her boss sent an e-mail at 9:01 a.m. "I didn't hear back regarding my request for the charity donors list yesterday. Please advise." Her heart ached for a moment. She quickly pulled the list with the right criteria from the database, alphabetized it, and printed it with the header the way her boss liked it.

As Susan handed the list to her boss, she said, "I'm so sorry for the delay."

Her boss smiled and said, "No worries." But she still worried.

During her lunch break, she drove to the mall, feeling nervous the entire way, as if all of the other cars were only moments from hitting her. She wasn't sure, but she thought she might be drifting too close to the line. She felt as if she constantly had to steady her car and right herself, as if her autopilot was set to "mistakes." When she got to the mall, she felt as if everyone was looking at her. A few men said hello. Since she was hardly ever in public without her husband, the sudden attention made her nervous, sad, and even angry. Susan didn't prepare to be looked at, and she wasn't prepared to say hello to anyone. She wanted to get back in her car, to just be alone. She wanted her heart to stop beating so quickly, to stop aching. "God forbid I had any real problems. How could I handle an actually difficult life? Everything is perfect, so why am I so upset?" she thought.

She felt guilty that she just couldn't be happy or at peace, even though her children were healthy, she was the last of her close friends still to be married, and they could pay their bills.

When she returned to the office, she grabbed a cup of coffee in the break room. She knew the coffee would only make her nerves worse, but she felt foggy, as if she wasn't thinking clearly. She overheard one of the staff nurses say, "I had a hypnotherapy session two weeks ago, and I haven't had to take Ambien since. I can actually sleep!"

That night, she and her family had a relatively nice dinner together with almost no voices raised. After the dishes, she started to worry around seven p.m. that she wouldn't be able to sleep. She knew that the thought of not being able to sleep made it harder to fall asleep, but she couldn't stop the worrying or break the cycle. She was about to get up for her melatonin when she remembered the mention of hypnotherapy at the office. She decided to make an appointment in the morning.

Three days later, on her way to the session, she was angry with herself. She couldn't believe she had paid up front for the session. What if it didn't work? What if she couldn't be hypnotized?

The hypnotherapist asked her a few questions, after which she closed her eyes. Susan imagined every part of her body relaxing, beginning at the top of her head. She relaxed her forehead, her jaw, and the tiny muscles next to her eyes. She relaxed her shoulders, arms, and legs, and she began to breathe deeply and slowly. The hypnotherapist counted backward, slowly, and for the first time in what felt like a lifetime, her heart began to feel better. The pain in her chest lessened and lessened until it was gone. She felt as though she could really breathe.

The hypnotherapist then told her to put her worries in a box at night, where she could always sort through them and pick out whatever she'd like to work on, one at a time. In the bedroom, however, worries would be prohibited. They were to be placed in the box. The box was to stay outside the bedroom, perhaps on the mantle or under a chair. "I'll put it in the pantry," she told the hypnotherapist.

"Very good. That's exactly right," the hypnotherapist responded. "Now that you've put the box in the pantry, it's easy and effortless for you to fall asleep. It's easy and effortless for you to fall asleep at night. You sleep easily and effortlessly through the night. If you happen to get up to use the bathroom, you'll fall right back asleep as soon as your head touches your pillow. It's easy and effortless for you to sleep. You have a wonderful night's sleep, and because of this, you wake up the next day feeling completely rested, clearheaded, happy, and full of energy. It's easy and effortless for you to sleep now."

After her session, Susan went home and had her best night's sleep since she was a child. When she woke up the next morning, the first thing she noticed was that her heart felt better. She thought about her children and smiled. She turned toward her still sleeping husband and didn't say a thing.

As she was brushing her teeth, she looked at herself in the mirror. Today was going to be a better day.

## How Taking Responsibility for Your Thoughts Differs from Affirmations

What you're going to learn in this chapter is how to choose better thoughts. At first glance, this might sound a lot as though we're headed down the road of daily affirmations, but we're not. Everything about the Close Your Eyes, Get Free process is about accessing and transforming your *sub*conscious mind directly. Daily affirmations are fabulous, but they only directly reach the level of the *conscious* mind, which means it takes a long, *long* time for them to impact your subconscious. Anyone who has practiced them knows it. You might feel better for a short time, but the underlying issue remains unless you repeat those bad boys six hundred times per day for a week (at least). Typically, people give up well before that happens.

The difference here is that we use hypno-affirmations during our self-hypnosis scripts, which means that you have already reached the theta brain wave state before we begin the conditioning process. Because you have already reached your subconscious mind, where your thoughts, habits, and beliefs reside, much less repetition is required. Usually ten to twenty-one repetitions per day does the trick. This is the difference between taking the Concorde to get where you're going, or a rowboat; affirmations on their own might get you there, but affirmations used during a hypnosis session are a much faster, smoother ride.

We've covered affirmations, now let's discuss vision boards. They're powerful, but looking at a picture of a house with a pool and tennis courts all day long isn't going to get you that house if your subconscious beliefs are "It's unsafe to be rich" or "I'm not smart enough, and I can't do it." It's like having a hidden Mount Everest of limiting beliefs that you have to traverse before your actions will match your desired outcome.

What you'll learn here is that hypnotherapy, and specifically the Close Your Eyes, Get Free process, will clear the way for vision boards, affirmations, and every other awesome Law of Attraction tool to be infinitely more powerful and effective.

In this chapter, I'm going to show you, step by step, the exact process that I've been using for years to live my best life and overcome habits that drove me nuts for a long time. We all know that if just taking responsibility for our actions were enough, every time we read a book and felt inspired by the action steps, we would actually do them for a lifetime. When was the last time that happened in your life?

There's something that comes *before* our actions and it gets in their way. It's our thoughts. Remember that we're working our way backward from what's most obvious—the actions, to what's most subtle—our subconscious beliefs. Right now, we're smack dab in the middle, at our conscious thoughts.

Have you ever wondered why, for example, when you really want to finish a project, you procrastinate? We've actually been conditioned to procrastinate, to have fear, and to doubt that we can be successful. Why do people who know that smoking is unhealthy continue to smoke? They really want to quit, but they haven't been able to do it. No matter how much we want to change, no matter how many books we read, and no matter how many seminars we attend, unless we meet those beliefs where they live in the subconscious mind, they can never change for the long run. Let's get some practical application under your belt so that the mechanism behind it makes even more sense later on.

Attempting to change a subconscious belief through conscious action is like trying to clean the bottom of the ocean by vacuuming inside your living room. It's never going to happen. You can vacuum until the floorboards have been worn thin, and you'll still never reach the depths of the ocean.

So, you might be asking yourself now, "How the heck do I accomplish this reconditioning? Is there something wrong with me?" And as I said in Chapter 5, this isn't your fault. We've all been conditioned for 20, 30, 40, 50, or 60 years, depending on our age. So, no matter how badly you want a change, to truly accomplish it, we also have to recondition our mind in the same way that it was conditioned in the first place. Our subconscious mind can be either our greatest ally or our worst enemy, depending on its conditioning.

The bottom line is that we have to take responsibility for our mind-set. Our thoughts result in actions, but the thoughts themselves have energy behind them. Thoughts are extremely powerful. It's vital that we take responsibility for our thoughts because the actions can only get us so far. Our mind-set is the first step toward creating our best life.

What happens if we start taking great actions, but our thoughts are still negative? There's a distance between what we're doing in the world and what we're thinking, and that creates a lot of tension and frustration. For example, "I'm taking responsibility for my actions, but there's still so much negativity in my mind. What's going on here? I'm so mad at myself for continuing to think thoughts that aren't good for me."

If you're experiencing this, it's okay. Frequently, when you first become aware of something like this, it seems to get worse before it gets better. This is simply because you're more aware of it. So, take a nice, deep, letting-go breath, and allow yourself to become aware of the fact that you're in excellent company when you decide to improve your thoughts.

·········· **A FEW THOUGHTS ON THOUGHTS** ··········

Luminaries throughout time have said some fascinating things about our thoughts and the mind. Here are a few to inspire you as you begin to take responsibility for what you think:

**Aristotle:** "The energy of the mind is the essence of life."

**Earl Nightingale:** "Whatever we plant in our subconscious mind and nourish with repetition and emotion will one day become a reality."

**Albert Einstein:** "Physical concepts are free creations of the human mind and are not, however it may seem, uniquely determined by the external world."

**Charlie Chaplin:** "Even when I was in the orphanage, when I was roaming the street trying to find enough to eat, even then I thought of myself as the greatest actor in the world, I had to feel the exuberance that comes from utter confidence in yourself. Without it, you go down to defeat."

Clearly, this concept that our thoughts create our external world has been around since the beginning of philosophical discussion. We're simply adding a fresh coat of paint and some deeper context to it.

It's all well and good to know that our thoughts create our external world, but if our thoughts are involuntarily negative, this information simply adds anxiety to an already overwhelming sense of powerlessness. We need to know both that our thoughts create our world *and* how to choose our repeated, habitual thoughts so that they're in alignment with our goals, dreams, and ethics.

# The Frequency of Power

After having read the last chapter, you now understand that by taking responsibility, you're taking a position of power. When you do this again and again, you begin to build a habit as a powerful individual. This brings us to the discussion of frequency.

There are certain frequencies that only dogs can hear. There are certain UV rays that only cats can see. They operate at a different frequency, as if there's a secret station on the radio that only cats and dogs know how to tune into.

Some people can run multiple billion-dollar businesses, whereas others seem to accomplish very little over the course of an entire lifetime. As human beings, we have the same skeletal system, cellular makeup, and structure of the brain. The difference is that people operate at different frequencies. It comes down to the difference in the frequency of the thoughts in individuals' minds.

Imagine two people growing up in the same exact conditions. Perhaps they're from the same town, the marital status of their parents is the same, and the median income of their home is about the same. But one person thinks again and again, "There are endless opportunities," and actually finds those opportunities. The frequency opens the knowingness, and that person walks through the door straight into those opportunities.

The other person from the same general upbringing says, "The economy is bad, no one's hiring, and there are no opportunities." Because this is what this person thinks, these negative expectations turn out to be true as well.

Your frequency of thought determines the lens through which you view your life, and this impacts the actions you take. Which frequency do you choose to live in? If you want to live in the highest frequency but you're still bombarded by negative thoughts, it's time to get excited, because shifting that pattern is what this chapter is all about.

It's important to understand, however, that although our thoughts are creating our reality, not every thought has an earth-shattering impact on our life. Having a thought in one energetic direction and a contradictory thought a few moments later more or less cancels out the first thought and the net sum for the two thoughts is zero. A positive thought plus a negative thought means there's neutrality, stagnation, and nothing moving forward. A negative plus a negative thought sends you backward. And a positive plus a positive thought means progress and moving forward. You probably have heard this before, but it's worth repeating: we become what we think about. Our thoughts become things, yet we still continue to take mini-negative vacations to complain about our day or feel sorry for ourself. Any movement in the opposite direction either neutralizes your progress, results in stagnation, or causes you to go backward.

Thanks to such books as *The Secret* and authors like Esther Hicks, the Law of Attraction is fairly common knowledge now and the idea of keeping our thoughts positive so that we invite positive experiences into our lives is not that radical a concept. That having been said, complaining is a powerful habit that doesn't break easily and I find that, in the beginning of our work together, even my most wellness-oriented clients tend to naturally respond to "How are you today?" with a list of everything negative, rather than recounting the many positive aspects and improvements in their life. Take a look at this example of a very common scenario:

The Second Step: Taking Responsibility for Your Thoughts | 137

Sally wakes up with a smile on her face, stretches, and looks at her vision board; she eats a healthy breakfast; she's feeling great that she's in the right frame of mind for her day. Then, her mom calls and asks how she is. Because Sally is used to venting to her mother, she says, "I'm doing all right; everything is okay. My boss was annoying on Friday. My Tinder date on Saturday was awesome, but I haven't heard back . . . typical. And the check didn't clear, so I'm behind on my rent. I looked really fat in this picture my friend posted"; then, realizing all this negativity might just be attracting exactly what Sally doesn't want into her life, she quickly follows it up with, "But I'm determined to have a great day and be rich and in love and be healthy and happy."

Feel energetically the degree to which Sally either plateaued, stagnated, or went backward because of that ten-second complaint-fest.

Now, for a moment, just imagine the best life you could live. What would it look like? Imagine it now. What is your best life? Feel the emotions your best life evokes. What are the images? What smells do you experience as you move through your best life? What do you look like in your best life? What actions must you take on a daily basis so as to live your best life?

Now, these actions you'll take to create that life will be the result of your *thinking*, so here is the most important question for you to answer:

*What thoughts must you be thinking all day every day and every moment to create your best life?*

Become aware of those thoughts that you must be thinking now. Is it possible to spend one more dinner complaining about college loans or politics or your ex and truly move in the direction of living your best life? This is vitally important. Now, when you slip up, do you want to spiral down a black hole of "No! I just thought a negative thought. I'm going backward. Everything is going to get out of control. I'm not creating my best life"? Of course not! Every day in every way, you're becoming more aware of your thoughts so that you can catch the ones that need to be immediately weeded out. Then, you can immediately replace them with thoughts that create your best life. Remember: A negative followed by a positive is a neutral. Catch those old negative thoughts and immediately defuse them.

My favorite way to do this is to say or think "Cancel, cancel" immediately followed by a thought that moves me in the direction of my desired life. Try it now: imagine you have the thought, "Ugh, what was I thinking, I'm so stupid!" then immediately think to yourself or say out loud, "Cancel, cancel!" immediately followed by, "I'm so happy I've learned this lesson. I'll do better next time. I feel better already." This "Cancel, cancel" tool will help you quickly clean your mental slate of all negative thoughts and fill it up with thoughts that are in alignment with the life you desire to create.

Remember, this is just the Second Step to Mental Freedom. Simply training yourself to think positive thoughts instead of negative thoughts does *not* instantly create the life of your dreams, but without this step, transforming your actions is rendered nearly impossible. The conditioning of both your thoughts and actions are equally important parts of the equation that ultimately lead to mental freedom.

Let's go ahead and do a brief self-hypnosis process that will help to transform negativity and complaints much faster than through willpower alone.

# Self-Hypnosis Process:
# Stop Negativity and Complaints

I suggest reading through the following directions two or three times before beginning so that you will be able to follow along easily. Remember, there are video tutorials and audio recordings available to you at www.CloseYourEyesGetFree.com that will help you to become a self-hypnosis pro in no time at all.

- Begin by making note of your starting stress level. 10 = a full-blown panic attack and 0 = zero stress, no stress at all, the most relaxed a person can possibly be. Remember this number.
- Sit in a comfortable chair and place your feet flat on the ground, rest your hands gently in your lap.
- With your spine straight but comfortable, take 4 deep, slow breaths, inhaling through the nose for 4 counts and exhaling out the nose for 8 counts.
- Close your eyes and imagine gentle roots growing from the bottom of your feet down into the center of the Earth, grounding you.
- Imagine a color you love flowing in through the top of your head, all the way through your body, out the bottoms of your feet, and down those roots into the center of the Earth.
- Bring all of your focus and awareness and attention to the palms of your hands. Perhaps you can feel your palms tingling, perhaps you can feel your heartbeat in your hands, perhaps you notice a sensation of expansion in your hands. Just notice and breathe for a few moments

(you can choose whatever length of time feels best, about 30 seconds is my personal favorite).

- With your eyes closed, count down from 10 to 1, saying "I am going deeper and deeper" after each number: Ten, I am going deeper and deeper. Nine, I am going deeper and deeper. Eight, I am going deeper and deeper. Seven, I am going deeper and deeper. Six, I am going deeper and deeper. Five, I am going deeper and deeper. Four, I am going deeper and deeper. Three, I am going deeper and deeper. Two, I am going deeper and deeper. One, I am going deeper and deeper . . .

- With your eyes closed, repeat the following hypno-affirmations silently in your mind or out loud, 10 times: I release all negativity. My thoughts are positive. I embrace happiness.

- Take another nice, deep, letting-go breath and with your eyes closed imagine replacing all negative thoughts in your mind with positive thoughts for the rest of your day until you curl up into bed tonight.

- Once you've spent 1–2 minutes imagining the rest of your day filled with positive thoughts and seeing the good in every situation, imagine the same color as before flowing in through the top of your head, all the way through your body, out the bottoms of your feet, and down those roots into the center of the Earth.

- Put a gentle smile on your lips, open your eyes, stretch your arms over the top of your head, and say, "Yes!"

- Notice your new number on the scale (remember 0 = zero stress, the most relaxed you can be) and congratulate yourself on how quickly you improved your state!

Here is a simple summary of the process in case you need to peek your eyes open at any point for a quick reminder:

- Notice starting stress level from 0 to 10.
- Take 4 deep breaths.
- Grow roots.
- Color.
- Notice your palms.
- Count down from 10 to 1 saying, "I am going deeper and deeper" after each number.
- Repeat the hypno-affirmations "I release all negativity. My thoughts are positive. I embrace happiness" 10 times.
- With your eyes closed, imagine thinking positive thoughts for the rest of the day.
- Color.
- Smile while opening your eyes and say, "Yes!"
- Notice new number on the scale of 0 to 10.
- Congratulate yourself for improving your state so quickly!

# Next Steps

Excellent! You have completed your sixth self-hypnosis process!

- Now, go ahead and visit www.CloseYourEyesGetFree .com to access this chapter's hypnosis recording. Pop in your headphones, sit back, relax, and Close Your Eyes, Get Free.
- After you listen to the recording, please let me know how it went! Using the hashtag #CloseYourEyesGetFree

on Instagram or Twitter, message me @GraceSmithTV your starting and ending numbers on the stress scale. By using the hashtag, you'll get to see how other readers are improving right alongside you, plus I will have an opportunity to cheer you on!

- Move on to Chapter 7 and continue to look out for all of the wonderful benefits you're already starting to receive as a result of learning the power of hypnosis.

## Chapter 7

# The Third Step: How to Reprogram Your Subconscious Mind

Mr. and Mrs. Cruz were having trouble in their marriage. The vibrant love that had been there in the beginning had, over the decades, faded into a worn-out, pastel gray. They lived in a beautiful town with low crime and great schools. Their two children had graduated and gone off to college with scholarships for both academics and athletics. On the surface, it all looked so good.

Although they were proud of how they had raised their children, they didn't know what to do with each other once the kids left. Without the endless homework, practices, and friendship dramas, it was as if a microscope had been placed over their daily habits. Every little thing each did seemed to the other like nails scratching down a blackboard.

Mr. Cruz hated how Mrs. Cruz never turned off the computer and refused to learn how to use antispyware software. He couldn't stand how her drawers always overflowed with bulky sweaters he felt should have been hung up, how she chewed gum loudly during movies, and how she always wanted to know how their investment portfolio was doing, even though she knew full well it had never fully recovered after the recession.

Meanwhile, Mrs. Cruz hated how Mr. Cruz would talk with food in his mouth, how he folded his socks, how he always moved her toothbrush from the shower to the cup labeled "toothbrush" even though she only brushed her teeth in the shower, and how he never seemed to hear her or care enough to truly listen.

However, they did have a few things in common. They each resented that the other didn't make more money, each disliked the other's friends, and were bored to tears by the other's hobbies (chess for Mr. Cruz and paddle boarding for Mrs. Cruz).

They were at a loss. They worried there was nothing left to fight for but always so much to fight about. The thought of divorcing at their age was terrifying, but so was growing old with someone who made them feel perpetually angry. Neither of them had done anything that was an outright betrayal of their marriage—no cheating, lying, stealing, or abuse. They felt ashamed that they couldn't even pinpoint why they were so miserable, but that didn't change the fact that they were.

They went to couples therapy, but Mr. Cruz felt like the therapist sided with Mrs. Cruz because she suggested they read *Men Are from Mars, Women Are from Venus*. So, they went to a male therapist, where Mrs. Cruz felt like he was siding with Mr. Cruz when he gave a knowing glance and said his wife also used gum as a way to de-stress.

The next Thanksgiving morning when the kids were home, Linda, their eldest daughter, mentioned that a girl she knew in high school had become a hypnotherapist. "Katie became a hypnotherapist?!" exclaimed Mrs. Cruz. "How weird! I always thought she'd end up on Off-Broadway or something."

Linda rolled her eyes, "Just because she was in the school play a few times doesn't mean she was going to end up on Off-Broadway, Mom. Anyway, we were all at the diner last night for a little reunion, and it sounds cool and like she's really helping her clients. Katie couldn't make it to the reunion, but a bunch of people from town have gone to her and told us about it. Sam got injured last season, and he said his pain level went from an eight to a four after working with Katie. If he focuses on what she taught him, he says he can make it a two. Laura told me she stopped smoking and lost twenty pounds after a few sessions, and Mary said their hypnotherapy saved her parents' marriage. Cool, right?"

Mr. and Mrs. Cruz shot each other a quick glance and both said, "Cool." Then, Linda opened the fridge, and the subject quickly changed to how someone had eaten all of the cranberry sauce before dinner. Mr. and Mrs. Cruz smiled, and their thoughts started to wander.

Two weeks later, after a lot of research online about hypnotherapy and a final "What do we have to lose?" Mr. and Mrs. Cruz found themselves sitting in the waiting room of Katie's office, feeling extremely uncomfortable. How could someone they had over for kiddie birthday parties help them? They didn't want to open up to someone they knew from such a small town, but they also didn't know where else to turn. The only other hypnotherapist was over an hour away.

Katie opened the door to her office with a big smile and said, "Mr. and Mrs. Cruz, I'm so happy you're here! It's wonderful to see you! Come on in." They all smiled, and Katie gestured to two chairs where the couple could sit. "Before we get started, I just want you to know that all sessions are a hundred percent confidential. Unless there's something criminal or dangerous I legally need to alert the authorities about, nothing leaves this office. There are so many wonderful families from town coming here that it's important for me to share that with you. If you've heard any success stories about our practice, it's because our clients shared them, which you're welcome to do or not do. But my confidentiality clause is simple—the hypnotherapist never discusses the session with anyone from outside of the session, ever. This means if you decide to have individual sessions at any point, what happens during those will never be discussed during our group sessions unless you want to bring something up."

Mr. and Mrs. Cruz let out an audible sigh of relief and said, "Thank you."

Katie smiled and said, "Now, what can I help you with?"

Mr. and Mrs. Cruz were amazed at how quickly they felt safe and comfortable during their sessions. Outside of a few neighborhood birthday parties, they hadn't known Katie all that well while she was growing up, and it was clear she knew what she was doing. But more than that, there was zero judgement in the air. After the first session, they felt so much lighter that they decided to add individual sessions. Over time, they found out that the things that drove them crazy about each other were due to years of built-up agitation as a result of completely unrelated events.

When Mrs. Cruz's conscious mind saw her husband chewing with his mouth open, her subconscious mind dug up every instance over the years when he hadn't loved, cared, or respected her and linked all of those to the chewing. The pair realized that a massive communication breakdown had taken place over time and that their marriage had taken a backseat to their kids and careers. They hadn't spent any time or energy on improving their relationship, but they'd spent a tremendous amount of time and energy complaining about it.

After some time and effort focused on healing their misunderstandings and painful memories, they laughed when Katie pointed out that one of their mutual dislikes was about how the other chewed, whether food or gum. They chuckled when they realized that the tension in their marriage wasn't about folding sweaters and socks, but about years of negative programming.

A few short weeks into their sessions, Mr. Cruz turned to Mrs. Cruz and said, "When you told me I wasn't listening or that I didn't hear you, you were right. I had actually developed a subconscious habit of turning down the volume, and I'm sorry. I can't imagine how painful that must have been."

Mrs. Cruz hugged him and said, "I didn't fully realize that by asking you about our finances multiple times per day every day that I was causing you pain. I realize now I had a subconscious belief that it was your fault we lost that money. Now, I understand there were so many factors, including the market, which was out of our control. I'm so sorry."

These kinds of breakthroughs continued as Mr. and Mrs. Cruz began to view their actions toward each other as habits that were programmed inside their subconscious mind, as stories that they strengthened every time they told themselves those stories. With Katie guiding them, they were able to write another story in which chewing, folding, and hobbies caused laughter instead of anger, and where deep appreciation could be felt deeply and expressed safely.

......................................................

## The Third Step to Mental Freedom

As you now know, mental freedom begins in the mind—the *sub*conscious mind. We've worked our way backward from the most obvious and outward manifestation of our subconscious programming—our actions—to the more subtle representation of our subconscious programming—our thoughts. Now, we've reached the source—the beliefs, habits, and emotions themselves. I hope that by this point, knowing that you have the power and ability to shift, form, and influence your subconscious mind brings a smile to your face. You are infinitely powerful.

Since you've been following along with the recordings as you read, I know you've already begun to experience profound and positive shifts in your life. This chapter will take all of that to the next level.

We learned in step one that taking responsibility for your actions gives you the power to make lasting change. You must have the desire to create change before any change will ever occur. Step two is to take responsibility for your negative thoughts so that you can immediately replace them with positive thoughts. Now we've reached step three, where you'll learn to recondition your subconscious beliefs so that they match your positive thinking. This is when lasting changes happen, and this is what makes hypnosis one of the most, if not *the* most, powerful tool available to us for personal change.

All of our conditioned behaviors are stored in the subconscious, yet very few people know how to access and change the subconscious. The truth is that your conscious and subconscious thoughts have to be aligned to create the life of your dreams. Once this happens, real, lasting change is possible.

*How do you know if your subconscious thoughts are in alignment with what you want consciously? It's simple: If you don't have what you want, your subconscious thoughts aren't in alignment with what you want. They're in alignment with what you were conditioned to think.*

Once our subconscious beliefs match our new and improved conscious thoughts, we feel a great deal of peace. Unrest, doubt, and nervousness can melt away because the false thoughts that produced them have been replaced by the truth. Of course, this doesn't mean it will never rain again, or that a person with horrible subconscious programming won't run for political office, or that someone we love won't face a tremendous challenge. The outside world continues to operate exactly as it always has, but you're far better equipped to handle it all when your conscious and subconscious minds are congruent and clear on what they want. When the vision is unified, there's a great deal of clarity about what to do.

Before you learn to reprogram your subconscious mind, you might have an idea of what it would be like to live the amazing life you desire. But inside, you just continue to *hope* that it will happen someday without actually knowing how to *make* it happen. Most people don't see the gap that needs to be filled between where they are and where they want to be. I'd like to suggest that you forget *hoping*, which might sound counterintuitive, and instead, align your conscious desires with your subconscious beliefs. Then, you can start *doing*. Even better, you can start *being* that congruent, balanced, peaceful, clear person.

## Why Positive Thinking Alone Doesn't Work

The number one reason why personal transformation often doesn't last is that nearly everyone is trying to make *sub*conscious change from *conscious* efforts. As I've said, it simply can't happen. Plenty of people on a conscious level have bought into the idea of the Law of Attraction, believing that our thoughts attract whatever we're thinking about. Plenty of people are careful not to complain out loud or to indulge in negative thinking, yet they're still exhibiting conditioned behaviors that don't contribute to living the life they desire.

This is my favorite analogy about the difference between the conscious and subconscious mind, so I've referenced it more than once. Imagine the conscious mind as a bouncer, and the subconscious mind as the people inside an exclusive club. The conscious mind's only job is to not let any new thoughts, habits, or beliefs into the subconscious that don't match what's already in there. If there are negative thoughts, more negative thoughts can get through, but positive thoughts won't be allowed in. It isn't the bouncer's job to determine whether these thoughts are helpful or will improve the joint, but only whether they match or not.

Affirmations alone, which act only on the conscious mind, are like taking a battering ram to the door of the club, and after thousands of repetitions, finally making a breakthrough and settling down at the bar. Hypnosis is like slipping the bouncer a hundred dollars so that the new thoughts can easily and effortlessly slip through the door and make themselves comfortable.

## Neuroscience and Thoughts

Sigmund Freud made the discussion of the subconscious and the unconscious mind mainstream in modern psychology. He used the analogy of an iceberg. The tiny part we see above the water is the conscious mind, and that massive structure underneath the water is the unconscious—the structure upon which the tiny consciousness sits. Every single belief we have is running constantly below the surface in the subconscious.

Every time we have a negative thought, it makes the neural pathway stronger, thicker, and deeper. Eventually, the thought can go from being a dirt path to becoming like a sixteen-lane highway that's deeply embedded in the neural network of the brain. For example, when you learn to drive a car, it's a very conscious effort at first. But after a few months, the pattern becomes so embedded in the brain that driving becomes subconscious. In other words, it becomes automatic. It's something that runs in the background while we talk to people in the car with us, daydream, or sing along with the radio.

When negative thoughts become subconscious or operate as an automatic program that runs in the background while we live our life, they impact our perceptions, interpretations, language, actions, and emotions. Unless we identify and weed out the subconscious, negative programming, we find ourself constantly struggling with negative conditions. The difficulty is that because subconscious programming is happening silently in the background, we can't *see* it taking place. More often than not, we accept these programs as truth and make them a part of our identity.

Now, remember, in the beginning, every single subconscious program was once nothing more than a seed of an idea cast in our direction. Eventually, these seeds grow into big, beautiful flowers or trees if they're congruent with the life we desire, or they grow into thick, ugly, thorny weeds if they keep us from aligning with our highest self.

While we aren't consciously aware of these programs, the subconscious and all of its programs can be observed when we deepen our awareness. As we discussed in the chapter on the science behind hypnosis, brain waves are produced by synchronized electrical pulses from masses of neurons communicating with one another. Brain waves are detected using sensors placed on the scalp; they're categorized into bandwidths so as to describe their functions and they're measured in hertz (cycles per second).

For a quick review, beta brain waves occur when we're awake, alert, and at our normal waking state of consciousness. They run the spectrum of 15 to 30 hertz.

Next come alpha brain waves, when we're relaxed, calm, creative, and perhaps doing some visualization work. They run the spectrum of 9 to 14 hertz.

Theta brain waves are deep relaxation, when we're in meditation, a wonderful state for problem-solving. They run the spectrum of 4 to 8 hertz.

Delta, the deepest brain waves, when deep, dreamless sleep takes place, run from 1 to 3 hertz.

The subconscious can be accessed and observed when we deepen our awareness of the mind to low alpha, any range of theta, and high delta brain waves—anywhere from 8 to 3 hertz. Once you deepen your mental awareness to these levels, you can observe how these core programs running beneath the surface dictate your perceptions, interpretations, actions, and everyday living.

As we've discussed, below the age of seven, human beings are pure subconscious. We're all little subconscious sponges in full-time alpha or theta brain wave mode, running around, picking up these seeds of beliefs from everyone and everything around us. But we don't just pick up words. We pick up opinions, behaviors, energies, color interpretations, feelings, gestures, beliefs—everything. We also interpret what we observe based on seven-year-old-or-less understanding, which is, of course, limited.

For example, if a five-year-old hears her parents arguing, her subconscious absorbs the following information: "The people who take care of me argue and fight." No matter how many times they tell her verbally that they are sorry she had to see them yell and that it isn't nice to yell, arguing and fighting still becomes conditioned in her little mind as a family behavior. The belief may look something like this: "As an adult, how you get your way is by yelling"; "As an adult, if you love someone, you yell at them." In terms of mimicking, children often pay much more attention to what adults do, not what they say. It's why the actual fighting between the parents holds more weight in terms of developing a subconscious habit or belief than their discussing how it's not nice to do that. Children are watching adults for lessons in "how to be a human being" and "how to survive in the world"; spontaneous repeated actions will always carry more weight than words said during a one-off carefully constructed conversation.

## Reprogramming in Action

Despite the fact that your subconscious mind may play a negative role in your life, it would never do anything to hurt you. In fact, your subconscious always believes it's helping you. In my first hypnotherapy session as a client myself, I found out that my subconscious mind truly believed that it was keeping me safe by making sure I stayed addicted to cigarettes. Somehow, I had absorbed the belief that when I smoked on the streets in New York City, I would come across as tough, cool, and unapproachable. Therefore, I would be bothered less by strangers.

My subconscious belief that smoke was like a cool, tough, protective blanket around me, keeping people away, became clear in that first session with a hypnotherapist. I was completely unaware of that belief until that day. Isn't that amazing? Let's face it: It's also a little scary and delusional, but the subconscious mind's job is not to make rational sense. It just wants to keep you safe and typically does that by continuing to do what it has always done.

Maybe my subconscious picked up that belief from a James Dean advertisement at some point. Essentially, my subconscious believed it was protecting me by keeping me a smoker when, in fact, it was endangering my health. I had to weed out that belief and replace it with a new, healthy one of my choosing. There's no way I would have found out or would have been able to deal with something like that from a conscious level.

## How to Create Your Hypno-Affirmation

In this next self-hypnosis process, you are asked to write your own hypno-affirmations by filling in the blanks. The more succinct and positive you can keep these, the better. Rather than using "I am free from thinking I am worthless" you can use "I am free from negative thoughts. I choose to believe in myself instead." Remember, whatever we repeat we strengthen so we don't want to repeat the words "I am worthless" over and over again, even if "I am free from" comes before it. We want to strengthen "I believe in myself." I want to make sure this is an easy step for you, so here are a few examples:

- I am free from overeating. I choose healthy portion sizes instead. I am finally free.
- I am free from smoking. I choose sipping water instead. I am finally free.
- I am free from fear. I choose flying calmly instead. I am finally free.
- I am free from fear. I choose speaking in public confidently instead. I am finally free.

If you have questions about how to make your hypno-affirmation the best it can be, just send me a message on social media @Grace SmithTV, using the hashtag #CloseYourEyesGetFree and I'll do my best to respond! You'll also get to see the hypno-affirmations other readers have written and you might find that they're just what you need. Ultimately though, as long as you fill in the first blank of what you want to be free from and fill in the second blank with something positive that will move you in the direction of the life of your dreams, you can't go wrong—have fun with this!

## Self-Hypnosis Process: Releasing Bad Habits

For this chapter's self-hypnosis process, I'll ask that you decide in advance one area of your life that you would like to improve; that will be the topic for this process. I recommend starting with just one topic in mind, be it smoking, overeating, nail-biting, fear of flying, and so on, and sticking with that one topic for twenty-one days or until you're seeing the results you are looking for. It's better to give your focus, awareness, and attention to creating one strong new network of neural connections about a particular topic, rather than creating a bunch of weaker, unrelated connections by trying to focus on too many topics at once. Once you see the results you're looking for, by all means move on to the next topic.

I suggest reading through the following directions two or three times before beginning so that you will be able to follow along easily. Remember, there are video tutorials and audio recordings available to you at www.CloseYourEyesGetFree.com that will help you to become a self-hypnosis pro in no time at all.

- Begin by making note of your starting stress level. 10 = a full-blown panic attack and 0 = zero stress, no stress at all, the most relaxed a person can possibly be. Remember this number.
- Sit in a comfortable chair and place your feet flat on the ground, rest your hands gently in your lap.

- With your spine straight but comfortable, take 4 deep, slow breaths, inhaling through the nose for 4 counts and exhaling out the nose for 8 counts.
- Close your eyes and imagine gentle roots growing from the bottom of your feet down into the center of the Earth, grounding you.
- Imagine a color you love flowing in through the top of your head, all the way through your body, out the bottoms of your feet, and down those roots into the center of the Earth.
- Bring all of your focus and awareness and attention to the palms of your hands. Perhaps you can feel your palms tingling, perhaps you can feel your heartbeat in your hands, perhaps you notice a sensation of expansion in your hands. Just notice and breathe for a few moments (you can choose whatever length of time feels best, about 30 seconds is my personal favorite).
- With your eyes closed, count down from 10 to 1, saying "I am going deeper and deeper" after each number: Ten, I am going deeper and deeper. Nine, I am going deeper and deeper. Eight, I am going deeper and deeper. Seven, I am going deeper and deeper. Six, I am going deeper and deeper. Five, I am going deeper and deeper. Four, I am going deeper and deeper. Three, I am going deeper and deeper. Two, I am going deeper and deeper. One, I am going deeper and deeper . . .
- With your eyes closed, repeat the following hypno-affirmations silently in your mind or out loud, 10 times: I am free from ____ [insert the bad habit]. I choose ____ [the opposite of the bad habit] instead. I am finally free.
- Take another nice, deep, letting-go breath and with your

eyes closed imagine being completely free from that old bad habit and replacing it with a wonderful new habit, for the rest of your day until you curl up into bed tonight.

- Once you've spent 1–2 minutes imagining the rest of your day filled with this wonderful new habit, imagine the same color as before flowing in through the top of your head, all the way through your body, out the bottoms of your feet, and down those roots into the center of the Earth.
- Put a gentle smile on your lips, open your eyes, stretch your arms over the top of your head, and say, "Yes!"
- Notice your new number on the scale (remember 0 = zero stress, the most relaxed you can be) and congratulate yourself on how quickly you improved your state!

Here is a simple summary of the process in case you need to peek your eyes open at any point for a quick reminder:

- Notice starting stress level from 0 to 10.
- Take 4 deep breaths.
- Grow roots.
- Color.
- Notice your palms.
- Count down from 10 to 1 saying, "I am going deeper and deeper" after each number.
- Repeat the hypno-affirmations "I am free from _____ [insert the bad habit]. I choose _____ [the opposite of the bad habit] instead. I am finally free free." 10 times.
- With your eyes closed, imagine that old bad habit is gone and has been replaced by a wonderful new habit.

- Color.
- Smile while opening your eyes and say, "Yes!"
- Notice new number on the scale of 0 to 10.
- Congratulate yourself for improving your state so quickly!

# Next Steps

Excellent! You have completed your seventh self-hypnosis process!

- Now, go ahead and visit www.CloseYourEyesGetFree .com to access this chapter's hypnosis recording. Pop in your headphones, sit back, relax, and Close Your Eyes, Get Free.
- After you listen to the recording, please let me know how it went! Using the hashtag #CloseYourEyesGetFree on Instagram or Twitter, message me @GraceSmithTV your starting and ending numbers on the stress scale. Please also share with me what habit you're letting go of and what wonderful new habit you're replacing it with. By using the hashtag, you'll get to see how other readers are improving right alongside you, plus I will have an opportunity to cheer you on!
- Move on to Chapter 8 and keep a lookout for all of the wonderful benefits you're no doubt experiencing as a result of learning the power of hypnosis.

# Chapter 8

# The Fourth Step: Giving Back

Michael's palms were sweaty, his heart was beating too loudly, and his thoughts weren't what they needed to be. He knew his pattern. If he won the first two matches, he would win everything. No one could touch him. If he lost one and won one, anything could happen. He had never recovered from losing the first two matches, and that's exactly where he was at that moment—two down. His coach knew it, too, and was already cursing, pacing back and forth, and running his hands through his hair every other word. "Tennis is a mental game! You need to know you can win this despite what happened in the first two matches. Your body is trained for this! Michael, you need to get your mind on board. You need to get your head in the game. We've come too far!"

All of the money Michael had saved from working at the deli the past summer was gone, spent on strings, rackets, and shoes. All he could think about was what a waste it had all been. His mind was filled with the grossness of the deli counter, covered in stale cream cheese, and how everyone came in from the town lake nearby. They would be tan and salty, and he noticed how pale his hands looked as he handed them their lunch. All of this was set to a soundtrack of his parents yelling.

During his entire childhood, his divorced parents fought over the cost of lessons and the traveling from tournament to tournament. It had seemed worth it when he received scholarship offers to all his top choice schools. But he was sure it was all about to vanish and all those fights, all that money, and all those hours spent practicing or working instead of going to the lake like everyone else would have been for nothing.

And Michael was right. After losing the next match, he was out of the tournament, and his school's last chance of placing that season was over. The ride back to campus was somber. The other players were angry with him. His knees were acting up again, and there was a shooting pain every few minutes in his shoulder. He started to think the thoughts he had every time he lost. "I had straight A's in school. I don't have to do this." But as soon as he was back on the court and once he heard that perfect "pop" of the ball on his 120 mile/per hour serve, those thoughts would give way to, "No one can touch me. I love this!"

The next morning at practice, for the first time ever, the good thoughts never came. He gave it a week, but they didn't come back. The love of the game had also vanished along with his hopes for a winning season. He called his parents to announce that he was quitting. He knew they would revoke his athletic scholarship, which was twice that of any academic scholarship offered. So, he sent in his application to a community college back home. His coach was both angry and relieved. On a good day, this student was better than anyone who had ever played on their team in the eighty-year history of the college, but the coach needed players he could count on consistently.

On the way out of the gym for the last time, Michael's coach said to him, "You have the potential to be great. Henry Ford said, 'Whether you think you can or whether you think you can't, you're right.' What that means is your only limitation is your mind. You had better learn that, son, or your life will be nowhere near as bright as it could have been."

It was two years before Michael picked up a racquet again. A friend's father from the community college threw a graduation party for their class at a fancy tennis club. As soon as he walked through the gates, he felt at home. The minute his hand touched the racquet, he felt a rush of adrenaline, and he knew it: "No one can touch me." No one there knew his history with the sport. They watched in awe as the sleeping tiger came to life, first beating all of the students, then the club members, and finally tying the club's head instructor. He was on fire, he felt alive, and almost immediately thereafter, he felt deep regret for having given up tennis.

The instructor walked toward the net to shake Michael's hand, "Awesome volley, man! You could have gone pro. Why didn't you?"

He looked into the instructor's eyes and said, "My mental game was weak. I gave it up after letting down my team at nationals."

The instructor turned serious, yet sincere, and said, "That's such a shame. Come by tomorrow. Here's a guest pass. I want to show you a few things."

The next day, Michael was up earlier than he had been in months. He could barely sleep. Even despite the few moments of regret that kept creeping in, he felt alive. His favorite recurring dream came back, in which he beat Roger Federer with the girl who dumped him right before prom sitting in the stands. He was practicing his backhand movement the whole way as he walked to the club.

When he got there, the instructor met him at the court and said, "We're not going to play today. Come with me." Michael was disappointed but intrigued, so he followed. They went to the club's theater and sat down in front of the screen. The instructor turned to him and said, "I was never as good as you were yesterday. Even in my prime, I wasn't as strong, fast, or agile as you were after two years of not playing. But back when I was playing pro, I won a lot of games because I cultivated what I could . . . and that was my mind. The really fast, really strong players didn't focus on this because they could beat ninety percent of the rest of the players out there with what they already had. But once you get to the elite level, it all becomes mental. If you haven't been training for that . . . well, you know firsthand exactly what can and usually happens. I don't know why they don't teach this the first day of tennis camp when you're eight years old, but here it is."

The instructor got up and turned on the projector. An antiquated opening screen popped up with the title "Self-Hypnosis for Athletes." Surprised and a little annoyed, Michael turned to the instructor and said, "I saw a hypnotist once. They had a show at my high school in the auditorium. It was ridiculous. People danced around like idiots. How is this going to help me?"

The instructor's tone was both serious and motivating as he said, without taking his eyes from the screen, "What exactly do I have to gain by taking time out of my day to show you this for free?"

Michael blinked a few times and realized he felt like he was back with a coach. That felt good—someone to tell him what to do and how to be better. He had missed that. He smiled and turned his attention back to the screen.

The video taught relaxation techniques that turn off the fight, flight, or freeze mechanisms that tend to show up when you're losing or have made a mistake. It showed how to detach from the past and prepare for what's coming next through visualization, breathing, and hypno-affirmations. It taught how the body and mind can't tell the difference between what's imagined and what happens in real life. Imagining defeat is *actual* defeat to the body and mind, and they react accordingly. Imagining winning is actual glory to the body and mind, and again, they react accordingly. The video taught how to enter into a "flow state" where the mind and body are relaxed enough that muscle memory, reflexes, and something that even seems a little magical—intuition—can take over. It taught that this winning frame of mind—the mind that moves beyond defeat quickly and prepares effectively to win in the blink of an eye—can be etched into the subconscious mind. It can become part of the blueprint of who we are.

When the video ended, the instructor turned to Michael and said, "How have you experienced this already in your life?"

"When the first thought I have as I pick up the racquet is, 'I can't lose; no one can touch me,' they truly can't. Then, if I win, I feel it even more for the next match until I really do feel like it's just me and the ball and everything melts away."

"That's because the endorphins we release when we win prime us to win again. Confidence, joy, and self-worth all release chemicals that allow us to open up, loosen up, and trust ourself. Defeat, shame, and anger are all restricting emotions. We close off and tighten up. Our agility is diminished, and the mind begins to overthink. The thing is, you can 'fake it till you make it,' meaning that with hypnosis you can train your body to release the same feel-good endorphins before every match, even if you just lost."

The instructor continued to explain. "You have to train your mind rigorously and that flow state, the state of peak performance, can be available to you at all times. So, does this mean it works one hundred percent of the time? If it did, Serena, Federer, and

Djokovic would never have lost a game. So, it doesn't guarantee that you'll win, but with enough practice, it means you'll be in a winning state of mind when you start the match, which at your level, is where you *have* to be."

Michael was riveted, as the instructor made this hypnosis stuff sound even better. "Hypnosis can also heal injuries faster. There was a study done at Harvard Medical School that showed patients with hypnotherapy healed broken bones forty percent faster than the control group who didn't receive hypnotherapy. And you can use it to train your brain to be more strategic. If for nothing else, you can use it to detach from past mistakes and lost matches. Every time we think about a game we lost or a mistake we made, we strengthen that tendency in the mind. This gives power to the part of our brain that we need to strengthen in order to win and also to continue enjoying the game even in the face of defeat. I hope you'll use this tool every day for the rest of your life."

The instructor put his hand out to shake Michael's hand. "I can't thank you enough," Michael said. "You've given me my game back. Please let me buy you lunch for taking all of this time today."

The instructor smiled and said, "Another time; I have to go practice my own self-hypnosis. I recently started studying French, and after that, I have ballroom dancing with my wife. Without this stuff, I wouldn't have made it past one class. I was all toes. Now? Watch out *Dancing with the Stars*!"

They laughed as the instructor made his way to the door and out into the bright afternoon. When the door had closed, the young player smiled, closed his eyes, and took a nice, deep, letting-go breath.

# The Fourth Step to Mental Freedom

My promise to you from the very beginning of the book was to teach you how to close your eyes and get free—to experience mental freedom and help you overcome the habits that have been chipping away at your self-esteem for years. At this point, I imagine if you scroll through the comments found using our #CloseYourEyesGetFree hashtag on social media, the stories of transformation will already be tremendously profound. To say the very least, I'm so incredibly proud of you.

By this point, if you've been following along with the recordings at CloseYourEyesGetFree.com, it's likely that you already feel more motivated, and you've stopped attacking yourself with as much negative self-talk. You're feeling more relaxed, confident, inspired, you're sleeping better, and you've gained clarity about your life that you have never had before. At this stage, a few people typically comment that they felt very emotional letting all that stuff go. This is perfectly normal, and like everything else in life, it, too, shall pass. It's also very common at this point in your progress to notice that you're finally following through on completing work and projects that used to suffer from the habit of procrastination. That's a hidden benefit we haven't even discussed yet but will get to shortly. The truly beautiful thing is that I'm sure all of these improvements in your life are also already impacting the people around you for one very simple reason—when you focus on living your best life instead of fixing everyone else, you end up making a lasting contribution to this world. It's a benefit to everyone who spends time with you.

To prepare you for the fourth step to mental freedom, I want to tell you the story of Calvin. He was the first little boy client I had ever worked with. He was just seven years old and so nervous during our first session that his mom had to sit outside my office and knock the whole time just so that Calvin was sure she was there.

Calvin had a severe eating disorder that had caused countless medical problems for his tiny body. He also had such a plethora of anxiety issues that it was impossible for him to lead a normal life. He had withdrawn from all of his friends and all of the activities he had once loved at school.

During his second hypnosis session with me, Calvin was calmer and less nervous, but there hadn't been too drastic an improvement since the first session. I went home that night feeling seriously doubtful of my ability to help people. I kept asking myself, "Is this the right job for me? Can I even help anyone?" I felt angry about the state of a world where a sweet child like Calvin would ever have to suffer so much.

Calvin's mom called me the next day. "What did you *do*?" My stomach dropped because she said it just like that. No "hi" or "hello." All I could muster was an eloquent, "Well . . . um . . . uh . . . "

Calvin's mother interrupted. "Calvin stayed in class all day long without crying, he played with a few children during the day at playtime, he ate some breakfast that morning without any fuss at all, he said he was thinking about going back to swimming class, he said he missed you, and he wants to play Transformers with you, Grace. Thank you from the bottom of my heart. I have my little boy back!"

Again that night, I found myself feeling emotional but this time, my thoughts were entirely different. "Hypnosis is so powerful! *Everyone* needs this!" I felt renewed and inspired, just as I had after that first session with my now father-in-law, Alexandre.

Calvin had a few more sessions, and he continued to improve with flying colors. I can't begin to tell you the joy I feel knowing that he won't have to grow up with the negative subconscious programming he had when I first met him. He rid himself of those neuroses when he was young so that he would never have to watch them become stronger and more powerful over the years. Otherwise, those neurons would have continued to wire together into more deeply entrenched habits. This story brings us to step number four in our four steps to mental freedom—giving back.

## Think About Others

After working with clients like Alexandre and Calvin, I wanted to help everyone overcome the core issues that hold them back from living their best life, and I wanted to do it as soon as possible before those neural pathways got any stronger. I created something called Grace Space, a "Netflix" of hypnotherapy programs, so that instead of working with one client at a time, which is all I had done up until that point, I could provide thousands of people with full-length hypnotherapy programs simultaneously. I also started live-streaming free hypnosis every day on apps like Periscope and now to growing audiences on Facebook Live.

Through this work I realized something very important that I had known during my college years when I was active with Habitat for Humanity, but which I had slowly and somewhat systematically forgotten while working in corporate America—that helping others, without an agenda or any personal gain, is the most powerful medicine in the world.

Just to be clear, focusing on helping others without taking full responsibility for cleaning up our *own* mind and life is not anywhere near as helpful as taking responsibility for our own mind and life, even if we never help anyone else. That's why this is the fourth step to mental freedom and not the first. This is an advanced step.

It doesn't mean you need to be perfect before you can make a difference in the lives of others. I don't profess to be anywhere near perfect, but there's a tendency to hide behind "making a difference in the world" when our own mind is filled with negativity, hate, and anxiety. Once we've found a new level of congruency within ourself, taking that peace out into the world is powerful medicine both for us and the people we help.

Remember: Since neurons that fire together wire together, every time you think about your problems and issues, you make them stronger. Interestingly enough, this entire book up until this point has been written for you about you, the habits and beliefs you want to overcome, the incredible life you want to design, your programming, your brain, your emotions, and so on. Although this is all extremely important and helpful, what's one of the fastest ways to feel better? To stop thinking about yourself so much.

We all know that's easier said than done. We're all obsessed with ourselves! Every selfie we take and every heart or like we get makes us even more focused on what other people think of us because even more eyes are watching. I imagine as technology continues to develop, this tendency toward constant self-promotion and the cycle of constantly refreshing to see how many likes we have will only become more compulsive. Luckily there is an antidote.

The one surefire way to get you to stop thinking about yourself? Think about others.

Some people might say that altruism is inherently selfish, and I say, "Who cares?" When we help others, it makes us feel good, not just because we're helping others but because the conscious mind can't do two things at once. If your conscious mind is helping someone else, it *can't* be thinking about you or your problems. So, it feels good both because it simply feels good, and it feels good because it doesn't feel bad!

Just imagine going out for a day and helping someone in need—painting someone's home, reading to less fortunate children, volunteering at a soup kitchen, or making a documentary on your iPhone about how to help stray animals. It's impossible to feel bad for yourself when you're focused on helping others. Writing a check can be incredibly powerful, but as far as cultivating tools that help us get out of our own mind, scribbling down a figure and our signature are just not the same as getting out into the world and getting our hands dirty (once we've taken the time to get our own mind right).

The truth is that we need one another. Even with all the training I've had and with all of the clients I've seen, I still go to other hypnotherapists for help. We can't see our own blind spots because we're too close to the issue. We're so deeply embedded in the "story" that it can be extremely difficult for us to recognize that it is, in fact, just a story.

While writing this book, for example, I had to pull out all the stops of every tool I'd ever learned or taught. I realized that everything I created up until that point had a relative impermanence to it. I could delete the Instagram post, I could re-record the Grace Space track, I could edit or take down the YouTube video, and all of my live-streaming would be gone after 24 hours. But this book will be around *forever*. I told myself before I started writing that it would be fun and even "easy" because I would program my mind to believe that it was, and so it would be.

Well . . . when I had 20,000 words of the total 65,000 left to write, I couldn't see the forest for the trees. I was certain everything I had said and would say was absolutely ridiculous and couldn't help anyone. I felt ashamed about reaching out to my friends, even those who had gone through the exact same thing with their books, because I'm supposed to be the one who helps people overcome *their* stuff! I'm not supposed to even *have* "stuff" anymore, let alone find myself curled up in a ball on the couch crying to my husband that I was certain I needed to give the book advance money back to my editor because I was the worst writer on the planet!

The irony of writing this self-help book while I needed more self-help than I had needed in five years wasn't lost on me. When I wasn't crying, I was laughing or shaking my head in disbelief. So, what was going on?

I've seen this with my clients enough times to know that there are layers to our ascension. When clients first come to me, there are usually a few very emotional sessions early on, during which we clean up past trauma. After that, few tears are shed for a number of sessions as the client builds up confidence. Once the clients hit a tipping point with self-love, the tears come back, but now they're tears of joy. When that happens, my clients are elated, and feel as if they can do anything. They feel unstoppable, and it's true! This is usually followed by a big life change—the next step up. Then, what happens? This new level is . . . well, new! It's foreign, and the part of us that's supposed to keep us safe by making sure we continue to do what's familiar begins to freak out.

This book was the next level for me, and more than one meltdown ensued. The beautiful thing is that I know for sure that the calm confidence will be next, followed by tears of joy. Once my

TV show about hypnotherapy is about to air, I'll likely find myself curled up in a ball again a few times. And that's okay. (I'm manifesting here: If you've loved what you've experienced with hypnosis so far, manifest a TV show with me so that we can make hypnosis even more mainstream!)

Every time this cycle happens, especially if we know it's happening, the distance between sad tears and happy tears seems to get shorter, and the added benefit of perspective takes the edge off a bit. For a person who is truly enlightened, it appears these levels need not occur and that meltdowns are not a part of the trajectory. But, as I'm still decidedly not enlightened, I take solace knowing that my experiences of peace and congruency last longer now than ever. The meltdowns now pass quickly and are few and far between.

When the self-doubt did pop up, how did I break out of it? By shifting the focus from my own insecurities to you, the reader. Whenever I stopped asking my husband, "How does this sound, is that funny, does this make sense, do you think people will like it?" and started asking myself, "How can I best serve my future readers? How can I best provide them with the tools and information that will help them the most?" I could immediately get back to work.

The message here is simple: To interrupt the pattern of self-obsession, stop thinking about yourself so much. Get out into the world and make someone else's day better. It's the fourth step to mental freedom because it works like a charm and is an extremely powerful way to change your state of mind. The following script will help you redirect your focus so you, too, can give back as you get free.

# Self-Hypnosis Process: Helping Others

I suggest reading through the following directions two or three times before beginning so that you will be able to follow along easily. Remember, there are video tutorials and audio recordings available to you at www.CloseYourEyesGetFree.com that will help you to become a self-hypnosis pro in no time at all.

- Begin by making note of your starting stress level. 10 = a full-blown panic attack and 0 = zero stress, no stress at all, the most relaxed a person can possibly be. Remember this number.
- Sit in a comfortable chair and place your feet flat on the ground, rest your hands gently in your lap.
- With your spine straight but comfortable, take 4 deep, slow breaths, inhaling through the nose for 4 counts and exhaling out the nose for 8 counts.
- Close your eyes and imagine gentle roots growing from the bottom of your feet down into the center of the Earth, grounding you.
- Imagine a color you love flowing in through the top of your head, all the way through your body, out the bottoms of your feet, and down those roots, down into the center of the Earth.
- Bring all of your focus and awareness and attention to the palms of your hands. Perhaps you can feel your palms tingling, perhaps you can feel your heartbeat in your hands, perhaps you notice a sensation of expansion in your hands. Just notice and breathe for a few moments (you can choose whatever length of time feels best, about 30 seconds is my personal favorite).

- With your eyes closed, count down from 10 to 1, saying "I am going deeper and deeper" after each number: Ten, I am going deeper and deeper. Nine, I am going deeper and deeper. Eight, I am going deeper and deeper. Seven, I am going deeper and deeper. Six, I am going deeper and deeper. Five, I am going deeper and deeper. Four, I am going deeper and deeper. Three, I am going deeper and deeper. Two, I am going deeper and deeper. One, I am going deeper and deeper . . .
- (Optional Step) Next, take a nice, deep letting-go breath, open your eyes, and, if you are comfortably able to do so, pick up this book or tablet and lift it up in the air so that your eyes are reading at an upward diagonal angle. Simply find the line where a wall meets the ceiling in your home. That is approximately where you want the center of your book to be—this does not need to be exact. If you are looking up at a diagonal, you are doing this correctly. Read the following hypno-affirmations at this upward diagonal angle until you have memorized them: I focus on others. I choose to help others. I ask myself, what can I do for the world today.
- Once you have memorized the hypno-affirmations, put the book back down and rest your hands comfortably in your lap.
- With your eyes closed, repeat the following hypno-affirmations you just memorized either silently in your mind or out loud, 10 times: I focus on others. I choose to help others. I ask myself, what can I do for the world today.
- Take another nice, deep, letting-go breath and with your eyes still closed, imagine helping others for the rest of your day until you curl up into bed tonight.

- Once you've spent 1–2 minutes imagining the rest of your day filled with good deeds of helping others, imagine the same color as before flowing in through the top of your head, all the way through your body, out the bottoms of your feet, and down those roots into the center of the Earth.
- Put a gentle smile on your lips, open your eyes, stretch your arms over the top of your head, and say, "Yes!"
- Notice your new number on the scale (remember 0 = zero stress, the most relaxed you can be) and congratulate yourself on how quickly you improved your state!

Here is a simple summary of the process in case you need to peek your eyes open at any point for a quick reminder:

- Notice starting stress level from 0 to 10.
- Take 4 deep breaths.
- Grow roots.
- Color.
- Notice your palms.
- Count down from 10 to 1 saying, "I am going deeper and deeper."
- Hold the book on an upward diagonal angle to memorize the hypno-affirmations.
- Repeat the hypno-affirmations "I focus on others. I choose to help others. I ask myself, what can I do for the world today" 10 times.
- Imagine helping others.
- Color.

- Smile while opening your eyes and say, "Yes!"
- Notice new number on the scale of 0 to 10.
- Congratulate yourself for improving your state so quickly!

In this self-hypnosis process we added the fairly advanced step of memorizing the hypno-affirmations at an upward diagonal angle. Let's take a look at why this is a powerful hypnotic technique.

### Why do we lift the book up and memorize the hypno-affirmations on a diagonal before placing the book back down?

Our eyes tire more quickly when we look up for an extended period of time, which sends a message to our body to relax. Have you ever noticed yourself becoming very tired after staring at a computer screen for hours? You weren't chopping wood or doing anything extremely physical for hours; you were simply sitting and typing—so why the exhaustion? The eyes become fatigued from the lights, and when the eyes become tired, it sets off a chain reaction for the entire body to relax deeply. In fact, this is why the silly swinging watch was a staple in early hypnosis; it simply tired out the eyes of the client and gave them something to focus on. Reading at an upward angle has a similar tiring effect and it can be very helpful for anyone new to hypnosis to use this technique to relax nice and quickly. You will likely find that you reach the theta brain wave state much faster than before and that you relax deeper now that you have added this step in. That being said, we simply want to be relaxed, not exhausted, so we only lift up the book for the time it takes to memorize those three hypno-affirmations before placing the book back down and resting our hands comfortably in our lap. While lifting it up, the exact location of the book does not matter, so please breathe easy if you are not lining the book up exactly where the wall meets the ceiling; an approximation is perfectly fine. In fact, this entire step is optional, so if it feels like it's too much, feel free to omit.

## Next Steps

Excellent! You have completed the Helping Others self-hypnosis process!

- Now, go ahead and visit www.CloseYourEyesGetFree .com to access this chapter's hypnosis recording. Pop in your headphones, sit back, relax, and Close Your Eyes, Get Free.
- After you listen to the recording, please let me know how it went! Using the hashtag #CloseYourEyesGetFree on Instagram or Twitter, message me @GraceSmithTV your starting and ending numbers on the stress scale. Please also share with me three ways you plan to make a difference in the lives of others either today or tomorrow. By using the hashtag, you'll get to see how other readers are improving right alongside you, plus I will have an opportunity to cheer you on!
- Move on to Chapter 9 and keep a lookout for all of the wonderful benefits that, no doubt, you are experiencing as a result of learning the power of hypnosis.

Chapter 9

# The Root, Trunk, and Limb: Overcoming Procrastination, Overeating, and Other Common Issues

Ashley had wanted to become a mother at a much younger age than most of her girlfriends. She would always say, "Bringing happy babies into the world is the fastest way to a happy humanity!" She always thought she would be a mom by age twenty-three. She felt that was the perfect age. She saw the number twenty-three everywhere for years; it seemed to follow her. She thought this was a wonderful confirmation that she was meant to become a young mom. Well, she felt this way all the way up until her twenty-fourth birthday, which she spent without a partner and without a baby. It was then that the first flicker of doubt came into her mind. "If I was wrong about this, what else was I wrong about?"

Ashley's twenties seemed to drag on with few significant relationships and nothing to write home about. On her thirtieth birthday, she looked in the mirror and didn't recognize herself anymore. The vision she had of herself for so many years and the vision others had of her simply had not come to fruition. Her eyes were resigned, and her lips were tight. Her identity had been in crisis for so long that she finally said, "Enough. I give up."

At this age, all of her friends who had wanted to "wait until I'm older" were starting to have children of their own. She put on a strong face at all of the baby showers, but it was difficult for her. With every passing day, she felt herself retreating, becoming a bit more numb as it was easier to just paste on a smile and feel nothing. She tried to build a new identity for herself by teaching yoga but nothing was clicking like the idea of motherhood. She knew she was drifting through life instead of living it, but she didn't know how to change. One day, when she was setting up in the yoga studio, a pregnant woman came into the studio and asked whether this was where the HypnoBirthing class was taking place. "HypnoBirthing?" asked Ashley. "No, it isn't, but that sounds interesting! What is that?"

The woman laughed. "Oh, I'm not even really sure. But my sister-in-law took this class before her third baby, and she said it's criminal that it isn't mandatory at all hospitals. She said having her third baby was one of the most enjoyable experiences of her life. She's really not a dramatic person or a hippie or anything, so it was really weird. She's actually an attorney and doesn't like anything 'woo-woo' but my sister-in-law described her birth as 'peaceful and beautiful!' Can you believe it? She's so convinced all moms-to-be need to take this class that she gave it to me as my baby shower gift. So, here I am, lost, looking for the class!"

As Ashley listened to the woman, she felt something she hadn't felt in the longest time. Her cheeks were flushed, her ears felt tingly, chills ran down her arms a few times, and she felt as though her heart was going to burst with excitement! After a quick Google search on her phone, Ashley found out that the correct yoga studio was a few blocks away.

Ashley offered to walk the woman to the class so that she would be sure to find it, but also because she wanted to find out more. When they entered the classroom, Ashley quickly found the instructor, told her she taught yoga, and asked whether she could audit the class. The instructor welcomed her warmly and told her where she could find a seat.

The instructor began by asking who there had never experienced hypnotherapy before, and 90 percent of the class raised their hand. The instructor joked how the prospect of giving birth seemed to have a way of inviting even the most skeptical of women to sign up for something they never would have considered before. Everyone laughed, and the room palpably relaxed.

As Ashley looked around, she was thrilled to see the diversity of the class. Everyone came with a "birthing partner," yet every partnership looked completely different. Some families had a mother and father, some had two mothers, some birthing partners were the mother of the soon-to-be mother, and some were dear friends. She felt it was a beautiful testament to all of the different meanings "family" can have.

The instructor then said, "Who here thinks we're guaranteeing you a pain-free birth?" A few people looked around the room, and someone in the back cracked, "If that's the case, I owe you more money." The room erupted in laughter, and the instructor said, "I want to clear this up. Every birthing experience is different. Every mother is different. Every baby is different. What HypnoBirthing does is teach us how to relax into giving birth, to breathe through a process that's been in our DNA since the time when women were giving birth in forests without any help. Now, I'm not recommending you go pick out a comfy spot on the mountainside to have your baby. Modern developments in birthing centers, home births, and hospital births are wonderful so long as they meet your preferences. The point is, you already know how to do this, and your body already knows how to do this. The simple truth is, when we feel afraid, we tighten up. When we tighten up, the process becomes painful. When we feel pain, we become even more afraid and tighten up even more . . . and the cycle continues.

"In HypnoBirthing, we teach you how to relax, relax, relax, breathe, to trust your body, to trust your baby, to trust yourself. When you relax, you open, open, open, making it easier and often faster for your baby to come into the world. Do some Hypno-Birthing mamas report a pain-free birth? Yes, but not all. Through all our case studies, we tend to find the word *pressure* is a much more common description of the sensations HypnoBirthing mothers feel, rather than pain. HypnoBirthing is about returning to what's natural. It's about empowering you to make the right decisions for you as you develop your birth plan. It's about teaching you to work with your health-care providers to meet your needs. To be clear this is not an 'us vs. them' situation where we're the crunchy-granola radicals and they're the evil medical staff who wants to force C-sections on all unsuspecting mothers. Hospitals, nurses, and doctors save lives every day, and maternal mortality rates in the Western world are lower than ever before, largely due to advances in medicine. At the same time, not every woman needs Pitocin to induce labor so that the shift change can occur on time. Does this happen? Yes. Does this happen at every hospital? No. It's all about being an educated advocate for yourself so that you can build wonderful rapport with the people who will be by your side, keeping you safe, happy, calm, and open during this experience."

Ashley was hooked. After the class she ran up to the instructor and asked, "When is the next certification course? I would love to be there!"

"You're in luck!" the instructor answered. "The next class is just twenty-three days from now." Ashley broke out into a massive smile as she felt happy chills running down her arms. Maybe one day, she'd have a child of her own, maybe not, but either way, she could be an advocate for mothers and their babies. She could teach them how to experience a deeper connection and how to choose relaxation and openness over the fear. In short, her dreams were finally coming true.

..................................................

I wanted to provide a story about HypnoBirthing, created by the brilliant and brave hypno-pioneer Marie "Mickey" Mongan, because it is one of the most powerful uses of hypnosis and it is one of the areas I am most passionate about. We discussed earlier the use of hypnosis instead of anesthesia for dental procedures and cancer treatments; now with that in mind, allow your imagination to run wild with just how effective hypnosis could be during child-birth. A calm, peaceful birth is possible. As my HypnoBirthing instructor and mentor, Dr. Vivian Keeler, told me,

What if the day you give birth is the best day of your life? Imagine looking forward to a birthing experience that is filled with peace, comfort, and joy rather than dreading a birth filled with the stress, fear, and pain that we have been conditioned to believe is inevitable. There is more to giving birth than just the physical act of getting the baby out. There is an emotional and spiritual aspect that far outweighs the physical. Giving birth without fear and surrounded by love and calm results in a feeling of powerful accomplishment and infinite joy. All of this and more is possible with HypnoBirthing.

I've always felt that the lack of widespread access to hypnotherapy is a human rights issue and I believe that bringing babies into the world might be where this issue is the most acute. If you or your partner are bringing a baby into the world anytime soon, I highly recommend spending some time researching HypnoBirthing and watching a handful of success story videos. You might want to keep a box of tissues nearby; happy parents with happy, healthy babies always set off my waterworks!

## Dissecting the Tree

Something as profound as pregnancy and childbirth can naturally bring a supercharged magnifying glass to all areas of one's life including outward habits, day-to-day stress, and subconscious beliefs. It is a crucial time to take stock of the conditioning that has led us to where we are, and the conditioning we will need to become the kind of parents we want to be. It's why I've taken the time to further explain the phenomenal tool of HypnoBirthing in this chapter. That being said, while pregnancy is the perfect time to Close Your Eyes and Get Free on a regular basis, you don't need to be going through something quite so life altering to be able to alter your life. Whatever your life circumstances, you can choose to pick up that magnifying glass, look more closely at your life than ever before, and begin the journey toward the best version of yourself, today.

Over the years I've developed the concept that there are root, trunk, and limb "topics." We will now dig into what these mean. This is a system I have devised that makes the progression of transformation clearer to all involved. Put simply,

- Limb topics are the issues we can see. They are the physical manifestation of bad habits, such as smoking and overeating.
- Trunk topics make limb issues worse. When a trunk topic is exacerbated, so, too, are the limb topics, such as when increased stress and anxiety result in more smoking or eating.
- Root topics we can't see, but they are the puppeteer holding the strings. Heal the root issue, such as lack of self-love and lack of self-worth, and the rest of the tree heals, too.

I approach the result my client is looking for by first determining which limb topics are holding my clients back most. Limb topics are the *result* of a root topic. They're the physical manifestation of a problem we can't see. Common limb topics include:

- Smoking
- Nail-biting
- Overeating

- Unhealthy eating (not in need of weight loss, per se, but in need of healthier food choices)
- Procrastination

Root topics go deep. They're "unseen," and they impact everything we do, think, and feel. They're the neurons that have been firing together for a long time and are wired together. Their connections run as deep as the roots of a redwood tree. With their reach, they cover proverbial miles inside your brain. In my experience, there are three primary root topics, and they're all interconnected:

- Lack of self-love
- Lack of self-confidence
- Lack of self-worth

While all root topics can be summed up by lack of self-love, I do find it helpful to segment them out into confidence, love, and worthiness because it's easier for us to see them this way. For example one might draw the conclusions, "I didn't ask for that promotion because of a lack of self-confidence" and "I can see that I continually dated people who put me down because of my lack of self-worth" more easily than "I can see that I overate because instead of wanting to nourish a body I loved, I was trying to hurt a body I hated." Of course, these actions are all subconscious until we reveal them through the process of hypnotherapy.

Prior to hypnosis, the answers are more along the lines of "I didn't ask for the promotion because I didn't have time to update my resume," or "I dated that guy because he was so nice to me in the beginning and took such an interest in XYZ, which my ex never did, so I figured they were nothing alike," or "I over-ate because I loved food, and my job required me to take clients out for dinner all the time." The lies you tell yourself are simply a mechanism of rationalization. They're not actually *why* we do what we do.

In this chapter, we're going to go over the primary factors I've found in my work relating to each of the most popular "limb" and "root" topics. Before we dive into those, however, there are a few things, such as negative thinking, which are not so obviously a root or limb topic. I call that a "trunk" topic, because negative thinking is really the conduit through which a root topic becomes a limb topic. Two other very important trunk topics are stress and anxiety. When our stress levels go up, the topics in our roots manifest more rapidly in our limbs. Everyone has some combination of the same root topics, and everyone has the same trunk topics to varying degrees. But everyone's limb topics express themselves in a unique way.

We are now going to work our way backward, just as we did with the four steps to mental freedom, because it's easier to see and recognize limb topics than trunk and root topics. The latter two are buried deep "underground" in our subconscious mind, so we'll visit those last.

## How to Use This Chapter

In this chapter I will cover a few of the most popular limb top-ics that my clients have sought hypnotherapy for; however, there are literally hundreds of other limb topics that I will not get to cover here. Please visit www.CloseYourEyesGetFree.com to see the additional resources available for topics you may need help with that we didn't have the space for in this book. In this chapter I will also cover the core trunk and root topics. While I believe you could benefit from reading the entire chapter in full simply because something that might not apply to you may apply to a loved one or colleague, I understand that you're busy and time is your most precious commodity! If you need to, by all means skip the sections that do not apply to you and focus solely on the sections of the tree that most need your focus and attention.

## Limb Topics

Let's begin with the most common request I have. Now, this is not the number one reason clients come to see me in the first place, but once someone is working with me privately or have joined Grace Space, this is the topic that comes up most frequently when I ask, "What are all the areas you'd like to work on?" Procrastination is almost always on the list.

### Procrastination

The world we live in is becoming filled with more and more distractions by the day. Esteemed leaders in business have already said that our ability to focus is the highest predictor of success in the approaching decades. This is because so few people will be able to do it. This means future generations will be less able to focus than millennials. The fact of the matter is, an ability to focus will be the slight edge, the margin separating the elite performers from everyone else.

Isn't that interesting? That is not at all the message I grew up with. In Chapter 2 we discussed what I believe are the biggest factors to our subconscious programming as children, which I call the "three E's," but for now, suffice it to say that my "Entertainment" and "Environment" inputs did not train my brain to think focusing on a single task was the coveted skill I would need to cultivate in order to excel at life. While growing up, the images of "success" I remember from movies and TV were of impeccably dressed people who were multitasking like robots, getting everything done without breaking a sweat. I grew up knowing that admissions counselors at the colleges I wanted to go to the most didn't want me to focus on and excel at *one* thing. Oh, no. They wanted us to have great grades, to be great at at least one sport, to play a classical musical instrument in a way that would make a high school band director cry (Mom, why wasn't I allowed to get an oboe in fifth grade again?), to be running every club, to have perfect SAT scores, to star in the school play, and to have a letter of recommendation from a previous president of a small nation.

I didn't have *all* those things, but the pressure of knowing I was *supposed* to excel in all those areas did have me running around like a maniac, going from club meeting to club meeting and extracurricular activity after extracurricular activity.

The conscious mind can only focus on one thing at a time. The subconscious is taking in everything that happens all around you, processing it and storing it—the smells in the room, what the people behind you are talking about, the brightness of the Kindle screen, the sound of the pages turning, and so on. But your conscious mind, the one you're using right now to read this book, the one you use throughout the day to get your work done, can only focus on one thing at a time. That means every time you're focused on a project and your phone dings with an update from Instagram, when you take a "second" to look at it, your progress could be derailed for as much as ninety minutes.

Now, that's not necessarily procrastination. It could just be an unintentional distraction that threw you off course repeatedly. Either way though, you can say sayonara to that deadline.

Distractions don't just keep us from accomplishing our goals, dreams, and deadlines; they're expensive. According to CBSNews .com, "A recent study by research firm Basex puts the 'cost of unnecessary interruptions' in terms of lost productivity and innovation at a shocking $650 billion. Merlin Mann blogged about the cost of the e-mail 'ding!'; that little sound supposedly costs the U.S. economy $70 billion a year, according to the *Guardian*."[1]

So, even if we don't "have" procrastination, as if it were a disease one could catch (it isn't), we all have distractions, and they're mounting. The result of both giving into procrastination and giving into distractions is the same—getting less done than we wanted. In a day, this can add up to frustration or disappointment in ourself. In a lifetime, this can add up to deep regret and the memory of thousands of hours spent hunched over a screen.

If the result is the same, what makes procrastination different from giving into distractions? Motive. Procrastination is not a sign of laziness. It's a fear of failure.

The fear of failure drives so much of our lack of initial effort. Because the subconscious wants to keep us safe, the underlying possibility of failure can be enough to keep us in our comfort zone, especially once giving into that behavior becomes a habit.

Overcoming procrastination requires that a number of different areas of the subconscious be transformed or reprogrammed. For example:

- Train yourself to begin with the biggest, most important task of the day.

- Bring greater awareness to the habit, and turn the negative "automatic" switches to "manual."
- Reestablish what feels good. Instead of the distraction prompting the good feeling, link accomplishing the task with the boost of serotonin.
- Reestablish the view of yourself. Reclaim your self-worth! Program yourself to be your number one cheerleader.
- Learn to anchor taking action *now*, getting started *now*, and ending self-deception.

Instead of placing our self-hypnosis process at the end of this chapter, we'll add it here since Procrastination is by far the most pervasive issue I've seen to date.

## Self-Hypnosis Process: Break Through Procrastination

I suggest reading through the following directions two or three times before beginning so that you will be able to follow along easily. Remember, there are video tutorials and audio recordings available to you at www.CloseYourEyesGetFree.com that will help you to become a self-hypnosis pro in no time at all.

- Begin by making note of your starting stress level. 10 = a full-blown panic attack and 0 = zero stress, no stress at all, the most relaxed a person can possibly be. Remember this number.
- Sit in a comfortable chair and place your feet flat on the ground, rest your hands gently in your lap.

- With your spine straight but comfortable, take 4 deep, slow breaths, inhaling through the nose for 4 counts and exhaling out the nose for 8 counts.
- Close your eyes and imagine gentle roots growing from the bottom of your feet down into the center of the Earth, grounding you.
- Imagine a color you love flowing in through the top of your head, all the way through your body, out the bottoms of your feet, and down those roots, down into the center of the Earth.
- Bring all of your focus and awareness and attention to the palms of your hands. Perhaps you can feel your palms tingling, perhaps you can feel your heartbeat in your hands, perhaps you notice a sensation of expansion in your hands. Just notice and breathe for a few moments (you can choose whatever length of time feels best, about 30 seconds is my personal favorite).
- With your eyes closed, count down from 10 to 1, saying "I am going deeper and deeper" after each number: Ten, I am going deeper and deeper. Nine, I am going deeper and deeper. Eight, I am going deeper and deeper. Seven, I am going deeper and deeper. Six, I am going deeper and deeper. Five, I am going deeper and deeper. Four, I am going deeper and deeper. Three, I am going deeper and deeper. Two, I am going deeper and deeper. One, I am going deeper and deeper . . .
- (Optional Step) Next, take a nice, deep letting-go breath, open your eyes, and, if you are comfortably able to do so, pick up this book or tablet and lift it up in the air so that your eyes are reading at an upward diagonal angle. Simply find the line where a wall meets the ceiling in your

home. That is approximately where you want the center of your book to be—this does not need to be exact. If you are looking up at a diagonal, you are doing this correctly. Read the following hypno-affirmations at this upward diagonal angle until you have memorized them: I am safe, I am calm, I choose to be here. I easily complete the biggest item on my to-do list first. I am in the zone.

- Once you have memorized the hypno-affirmations, put the book back down and rest your hands comfortably in your lap.
- With your eyes closed, repeat the following hypno-affirmations you just memorized either silently in your mind or out loud, 10 times: I am safe, I am calm, I choose to be here. I easily complete the biggest item on my to-do list first. I am in the zone.
- Take another nice, deep, letting-go breath and with your eyes still closed, imagine being more productive than you have ever been until you curl up into bed tonight. See, feel, and experience yourself knocking items off your to-do list one by one. Have a smile on your lips as you imagine this.
- Once you've spent 1–2 minutes imagining the rest of your day being more productive than ever before, imagine the same color as before flowing in through the top of your head, all the way through your body, out the bottoms of your feet, and down those roots into the center of the Earth.
- Put a gentle smile on your lips, open your eyes, stretch your arms over the top of your head, and say, "Yes!"
- Notice your new number on the scale (remember 0 = zero stress, the most relaxed you can be) and congratulate yourself on how quickly you improved your state!

Here is a simple summary of the process in case you need to peek your eyes open at any point for a quick reminder:

- Notice starting stress level from 0 to 10.
- Take 4 deep breaths.
- Grow roots.
- Color.
- Notice your palms.
- Count down from 10 to 1 saying, "I am going deeper and deeper."
- Hold the book on an upward diagonal angle to memorize the hypno-affirmations.
- Repeat the hypno-affirmations "I am safe, I am calm, I choose to be here. I easily complete the biggest item on my to-do list first. I am in the zone" 10 times.
- Imagine being more productive than ever before.
- Color.
- Smile, open your eyes, say, "Yes!"
- Notice new number on the scale of 0 to 10.
- Congratulate yourself for improving your state so quickly!

## Smoking

There tends to be two kinds of smoker, as far as the subconscious mind is concerned. First, there's the one who connects smoking with something or someone else that's perceived as positive by the brain, such as a cool actor, a beloved grandparent, or a favorite teacher. This is becoming less and less common as the public perception of a "smoker" has taken a 180-degree turn in recent decades.

A hipster yoga teacher friend of mine living in Brooklyn coughed directly in a smoker's face in retaliation to the person's secondhand smoke and posted a video of it online. The post received so many likes so quickly that I was genuinely surprised. Just a few years ago, when I was living on the Lower East Side of Manhattan, all of my friends still smoked. Now, rather than smoking being perceived as "cool," "badass," "dangerous," or "sexy," it is perceived more often as a gross habit that controls the addict. That's a shift in perception, a massive reframe that was decades, if not centuries,[2] in the making.

The second most common subconscious reason for smoking is to "protect" us from something else. It doesn't make any conscious sense. Our subconscious rarely does before we start using hypnotherapy. But the idea is that if the subconscious links smoking with anything that's very important to our survival, it will continue smoking. For example, if smoking is linked to stress relief in the brain, such as getting out of the toxic office environment to go out and get some fresh air and some downtime, to take some deep inhalations and exhalations (even if they're filled with tar and carcinogens), then the brain will view smoking as a "good" thing. In my case, when I had my quit smoking hypnotherapy session, the subconscious "smoker" in me thought it was keeping me safe by making me look tough and unapproachable so that I could walk down the street in New York City without being bothered.

When we access the subconscious mind through the theta brain wave state of hypnosis and use something called parts therapy, where we can speak to different parts of the self, as if it is another person entirely, we very quickly learn the motive behind the continued existence of "The Smoker."

Once we understand why the subconscious believes that smoking is somehow helping, it can be as easy a conversation as explaining the physical, mental, emotional, and financial consequences of smoking to the subconscious mind. My favorite phrase is "I know you're *trying* to help me, and I know you're *trying* to protect me. But the truth is that you're hurting me." When the subconscious "hears" this, it takes the message seriously. After establishing how smoking cigarettes is worse for you than any perceived benefit, however, it's important to replace the habit with a new one.

My favorite is to replace smoking with drinking water. Many people have a fear of gaining weight if they quit smoking. By replacing the smoking with the act of sipping water, they're still satisfying the hand-to-mouth habit, but instead of food entering into the body, it's cool, clean, clear water, which has the added benefit of flushing out toxins.

We can take it a step further and anchor the act of drinking water to the feeling of calm, relaxation, and relief. A lot of smokers perceive their habit as a mechanism for stress relief. In fact, it's the opposite. The mental and physical addiction to nicotine creates more stress. Have you ever seen a nonsmoker dying to get through customs after an international flight, to be able to light up?

By anchoring the act of sipping water to the feeling of stress relief, you're taking care of the perceived (albeit incorrect) link in the brain to smoking and stress relief, while satisfying the desire for the hands to be brought up to the mouth multiple times per day.

Depending on how badly clients want to quit when they arrive, a few "cut-down" sessions can be really helpful before the actual "quit" session.

For example, clients can determine their number on the scale from 0 to 10.

> 0 = "I still love smoking. Nothing bothers me about it except my family/friends want me to quit, and I'm tired of them bothering me about it/tired of worrying them." At this stage, there's no internal desire to quit.

5 = "I want to quit for financial and health reasons, but I
    still enjoy smoking."

10 = "I hate the smell, I hate the taste, I hate how expensive
    it is, and I hate myself every time I light up. I'm SO
    DONE."

If you find yourself at a 5 or below, a few cut-down sessions will help tremendously. If you're a 7+ on the scale, you can likely go straight into a few quit sessions and see lasting success. Again, hypnotherapy isn't magic. It isn't about seeing if you can overcome decades of programming in one sixty-minute session. It's about having as many sessions as you need to see the results you want.

On average, my clients have stopped smoking with all cravings gone after three to four sessions, typically a combination of both cut-down and quit sessions. This means some quit with fewer sessions, and some require more. You may need one, two, five, six, or ten sessions to quit and you might need a session or two down the line to keep you on the straight and narrow. In the grand scheme, that's a very small investment of time and money to be free of an addiction that's causing so much unnecessary pain.

When I first started out has a hypnotherapist, a friend of mine told me he had been to a hypnotist who only provided sessions for smoking cessation. The hypnotist guaranteed you'd only need one session or your money back. My friend paid $500 for the session, stopped smoking completely (he had been smoking a pack a day for ten years), and then three months later, had a cigarette at a party when he was completely wasted.

His response to the experience? "It didn't work. I guess I can't be hypnotized."

Is this true?

No! He *stopped* smoking *completely* for three full months.

That's ninety days of no smoking, and then a relapse while drunk. What this means is the following:

- The hypnotherapist who marketed himself as a one-session wonder made clients believe it had to work in one session, which is false.
- Even with a three-month success rate, the client believed he couldn't be hypnotized, when he clearly had been.
- The effects of hypnosis target your subconscious mind, and your conscious mind helps to keep you on track. When you're impaired through the use of drugs or alcohol, the parts of the brain that were transformed during hypnotherapy are no longer running the show. Every single "relapse" I have ever encountered with any client of mine, ever, started with alcohol, pot, or another controlled substance.

So, what should you do?

- Have the amount of sessions you need in order to see the results you want. It could be one session, or it could be ten. It will still be faster and more effective than anything else you've tried up until this point.
- If you happen to slip at some point in the future, come back and have another session! If you're going to the gym every day and are seeing your body transform, but then one day, you decide to stay home and eat potato chips and start eating too much regularly again, do you say to yourself, "Oh, I guess the gym doesn't work"? No! To see

the results, you have to work the tool.
- Remember that hypnosis isn't magic, but it's likely the most powerful tool for personal transformation that exists today.

Avoid cop-out excuses, such as "I don't have the money for hypnotherapy sessions." Here's some tough love: Guess what? You would have the money if you stopped smoking. Waiting for it to show up before you get the help instead of allocating the funds towards the help *now* is not serving you. I've had weight loss clients mention this, too: "I'd love to have sessions with you, but my food shopping bill is extremely expensive." How is that ever going to change without reallocating how you're spending your money up front? If there are other ways for you to stop your habit without investing money in reprogramming your subconscious mind, you probably would have tried them by now. Did they work? Private hypnotherapy sessions are typically the most effective and rapid way to see lasting transformation to subconscious beliefs and habits simply because the sessions are uniquely tailored to you. That said, dozens, if not hundreds, of people have overcome their worst habits by listening to my Grace Space recordings alone. If you live in NYC the monthly cost of Grace Space is the equivalent to 3.3 packs of cigarettes. Getting your financial priorities in order could mean that your life looks drastically different much sooner than you ever thought possible.

In addition, I've put a sample Quit Smoking hypnosis recording inside the bonus section of www.CloseYourEyesGetFree.com. Combine this with any of the stress relief self-hypnosis processes found in other chapters and you'll be well on your way to a smoke-free existence without any additional investment at all. Huzzah!

## Overeating/Unhealthy Eating

Weight loss sessions are among the most popular topics within hypnotherapy. I have also found that nearly all of my clients, even those who don't need to lose a single pound, are very interested in sessions that help them make healthier eating choices throughout the day.

The important thing to remember here is Pavlov's dogs. Pavlov trained his dogs to salivate every time he rang a bell. To begin with, he would give his dogs food every time he rang the bell. Eventually, he removed the food altogether, yet the neurons that fired together for so long were wired together to the point that simply the sound of the bell elicited the same reaction that dangling a piece of meat over their cute little fuzzy heads had done.

For all of you foodies, prepare yourself for this section. I use language that may raise an eyebrow at first, but hear me out.

We're trained to eat absolute garbage from a young age. Food is anything that comes from the earth. It grows in the dirt, grows on trees, and is a natural inhabitant of this planet. Food nourishes our bodies. It's the fuel for our body machines.

Everything else is poison.

That's how simple I make it for our subconscious mind during my sessions on this topic. You're either eating food, or you're eating poison. Why would I do this? Why would I degrade the preciousness of a child's colorful birthday cake down to the level of a big pile of bug-attracting poison?

It's simple! We've been trained through birthday parties, graduations, holidays, Grandma's cookies, and "If you're a good little boy/girl, I'll let you have a treat when we get home" to associate sugary, carby, synthetic stuff with "I'm important!! I'm loved! This is the best time of year! I'm a good little kid!!" feelings. It's

Pavlov's dogs reverse engineered. Instead of taking away the food, we've taken away the whistle. Whenever we want to feel as special, happy, and loved as we did when we were given a cupcake for our fifth birthday, we eat piles of lasagne while binge-watching Netflix. Remember when I said the subconscious mind rarely makes sense?

Many eat to feel loved, or because it reminds them of someone they love, because they're bored, because there's food in front of them, or because they've developed a habit of eating. Do you think a session where I build up the delicious beauty of a Granny Smith apple but still allow room for Granny Smith's chocolate lava cake will win out in the long run?

My black-and-white approach of food vs. poison works like a charm because the subconscious wants to keep us *safe*! Before our session, the subconscious "thinks" that setting off those reward centers, the pleasure centers in the brain, with all of that sugar, fat, and salt is helping us, but it isn't. It's hurting us. For starters, it's keeping us fat, diabetic, sad, lethargic, and angry with ourself, which ruins a few other things, such as our productivity, sex life, ability to feel happy naturally, and general health.

If that still sounds too extreme for you because while you learn to make healthier choices and/or lose weight, you still want to leave space for the occasional slice of Key lime pie, take a look at what my client Julia has to say about her experience:

"First, I wanted to stop eating junk food. I'm healthy, fit, and knew that that was not something I wanted in my body. But I seem to have no control over the cravings. Goal 1: dropping junk food. Well, this has been a topic for me *forever*. After the first session, I began to see my craving thought process interrupted. I wouldn't just jump into a box of cookies. Instead, I would think about what was triggering that craving and perhaps meditate through it. Now, the first week, I did have some sweets, but not as many and only one day. That's a success right there! I listened to our session several times during the week—sometimes when I was out on a run. That was a great combination of healthy activity supported by healthy choices.

"The second session included an element of aversion, saying that junk food was poison and helping me to imagine how I needed real food from the earth to nourish my active and stressed body. I have a stubborn little girl streak, and this little girl was part of the narrative of my hypnosis. I was going to help myself by helping my stubborn little girl show herself (and myself) self-compassion by eating yummy, whole foods, and throwing away the junk food. In my hypnosis, I cleaned out all the junk food in my house. When I got home that evening, I did clear out all my junk food!!! Since that second session, I haven't had any junk food. It's not that I haven't had cravings. Instead, I make a loving, healthy choice for myself.

"All this great behavior is happening while at work. I'm working fifteen-hour, very busy, stressful days. But by nourishing my body well, I'm managing the stress, and we hadn't even done the stress hypnosis yet!!!"

Julia's story illustrates that once we show our subconscious mind what real food is, it becomes natural to make the loving choice for our body, mind, and life. The voice that says, "I don't want to give up junk food; I just want to eat less of it" is the mind that's still hardwired to believe that junk food = reward. When we share the truth with our subconscious mind, that our body is magnificent and deserves to be treated as such, that real food is fuel, and our body deserves only the highest quality of fuel, then saying no to gross stuff cooked up in a lab becomes the obvious thing to do. The sense of deprivation melts away and is replaced by the knowingness of "I deserve better."

Another example of how our subconscious mind can react to food-related hypnosis was showcased during my segment on CBS's hit show *The Doctors*. My wonderful client Karyn completely overcame her addiction to sugar, the root of which was tied to loving moments while baking with her mother as a child. The experience was full of tears and transformation. You can watch the segment and experience one of my favorite weight loss/healthy choices hypnosis recordings by logging into www.CloseYourEyesGetFree.com and selecting Chapter 9. I've also included a self-hypnosis script for weight loss in Chapter 10.

······· AVERSION THERAPY ·······

Aversion therapy is a tool used to create a negative association with something. I don't use it very often in my hypnotherapy sessions simply because it isn't always necessary; however, with overcoming addiction to certain foods it can be very effective. For example, I will have clients imagine chocolate or cupcakes—or whatever their vice is—covered in bugs, to create a gross association with something that used to have only outrageously positive associations (such as happy childhood memories, birthdays, rewards for good behavior, etc.) on the level of the subconscious mind. Does this mean that every time those clients see a cupcake from now on, they will run in the opposite direction, screaming in terror, because all they saw was a pile of bugs or a big hazmat container filled with actual poison? Absolutely not! Aversion therapy does not create new phobias and hypnosis does not create mirages. We still see exactly what is there.

The difference is, the clients will now have an aversion to the cupcakes, or no desire for them at all, because the subconscious association is no longer positive.

........................................................................

## Nail-Biting

Nail-biting, oh nail-biting. It's important that a hypnotherapist
never suggests a particular area is "difficult" to overcome because
it may be very simple for you to leave nail-biting in the dust. At the
same time, different topics tend to require different approaches,
as nothing is one-size-fits-all in the subconscious. It's important
to discuss these trends so that clients are empowered to seek out
the number of sessions they need rather than assuming, as in the
smoking example earlier, that it just "doesn't work" for them if one
session fails to produce the desired end result. Let me put it this
way: Many of my colleagues and I have noticed that most other
popular hypnotherapy topics tend to see faster and longer-lasting
results than obsessive-compulsive behaviors, such as this one.

"For many, biting your nails may seem like just an ugly habit.
Recently, psychiatrists are changing the way we will view nail
biters." . . . "the American Psychiatric Association's Diagnostic and
Statistical Manual of Mental Disorders (DSM) will classify nail
biting as an obsessive compulsive disorder (OCD)."[3]

Most people are very surprised by this! They assume quitting smoking would be the "hardest" case for hypnotherapists,
but why? Now that you've quit smoking, the cigarettes are gone
from your life. People don't walk around with an unlit cigarette in
their mouth all day, testing to see whether they will light it or not.
Once the beliefs have been transformed, it's actually quite simple to

remove the smoking paraphernalia from one's life, especially since smoking inside public buildings is now illegal. When it comes to weight loss, it's a little more involved than quitting smoking simply because you still need to eat so as to sustain yourself. We can't simply throw all food away for good as we would an ashtray. That said, it's fairly straightforward to throw "poisonous" foods away and to fill your home and lunch bag with foods that nourish your body.

When it comes to nail-biting, our fingers aren't going anywhere, and there's always a fresh supply of nails every few days.

In that way, it might be safe to assume that the approach per topic could be determined by how quickly we can distance ourself from all factors related to the habit. An alcoholic is advised to remove all alcohol from the house. Why live with temptation in sight? For the person who doesn't have that luxury and will forever live attached to "the culprit," regular "upkeep" sessions are tremendously helpful in staying on track.

Is it possible to stop OCD-related habits altogether with hypnosis? Has it been done? Absolutely! Clients who seek out hypnotherapy for nail-biting, skin picking, pulling out eyelashes, and more have reported lasting results. Similar clients have seen results for weeks or months at a time and simply need to come in for a pick-me-up. Similarly, as long as enough sessions are done, there's always a measurable improvement and palpable relief for the client.

The story of my student Lisa and her daughter, Emma, is a perfect example of just how powerful hypnotherapy can be for any anxiety-based behavior.

Lisa wrote to me to let me know her daughter was struggling. "Last year, my eleven-year-old daughter Emma's eyelash pulling was at its worst. She had no eyelashes left, and she was getting small sores on her eyelids from picking at the tiny eyelashes that were trying to grow in. The eyelash pulling had become an even bigger problem than the aesthetic one. She was now feeling worse and worse every time she pulled an eyelash. She continuously told us how she 'couldn't stop' and that she was 'dumb' and 'not normal.'"

Lisa asked me whether I would be able to work with Emma on her self-esteem around pulling her eyelashes, and perhaps even the habit itself. When working with a child, I find it valuable to ask the parent what, in his or her view, a successful outcome would be, and then I ask the child the same. This lets me know early on if their goals are in alignment as sometimes the child isn't even looking for the result that the parent has booked the session for. I always, always keep the contents of my discussions with clients confidential, and children are no exception, so this is not something I report back to the parent(s), it is simply so that I will know everyone's point of reference when the work begins and it helps me to manage everyone's expectations.

Lisa said that her goal was simply to free Emma from the burden of how picking her eyelashes made her feel and that she wasn't concerned about the habit itself. Emma said that if she went from pulling five to ten eyelashes per day to pulling that many per week, she would consider that a success.

Emma and I then had her first hypnosis session over the phone. I recorded the session for her as it was very positive and instructed her to listen to the recording as often as possible. Lisa wrote to me soon thereafter with the following,

"Within twenty-four hours, Emma started noticing that she wasn't picking as many eyelashes! I also noticed that when she did pick one, she didn't seem to feel so bad. And she had just picked one! She usually would pick one, feel bad, and pick more and more. But she would pick just one! She continued to listen to the recording and saw impressive results!" A few months later, Lisa wrote again, "Now, six months later, Emma has some full eyelashes back, and more are growing. But most importantly, her habit doesn't affect how she feels about herself! She is happy and carefree again and not focused on how many eyelashes she has or doesn't have! It's truly amazing! Emma has carefree childhood freedom back and I am so very grateful for that!"

Remember when I said it very well may be easy and effortless for you to leave your habit in the dust very quickly? Emma just had the one session, but had she needed more, I know her mom would have booked those sessions. Whenever I think about Emma, I tear up. Imagine if Lisa hadn't called me simply because she believed hypnosis was just for stage show stuff or that it was the creepy mind control portrayed in movies, such as *Get Out*. How needless Emma's ongoing suffering would have been.

Emma closed her eyes and got free at eleven years old. How magnificent is that? Magnificent enough for me to continue this journey until hypnosis is mainstream? Damn straight. The icing on the cake? Lisa is now studying with me to be a hypnotherapist herself! She's just as fabulous a student as she is a mother, and it's a joy to have her in class. Thank you, Lisa!

## Trunk Topics

Trunk topics are the conduits through which our hidden root topics show themselves to the world via visible limb topics. The more someone experiences a trunk topic, the "worse" the limb topics tend to become. For example, the more stressed we are, the more we tend to bite our nails, eat, smoke, and procrastinate. The more negative thoughts we think about ourself, the more likely we're willing to express our limb topics.

Trunk topics are also interrelated. For example, as our stress levels go up, typically so do our negative thoughts. When our negative thoughts increase, it's likely that our stress and anxiety also increase.

## Negative Thinking

Negative thinking is a habit. If you think negative thoughts chronically, you're not a negative person. Your brain is simply trained to think negative, heavy thoughts, and it can be trained to lighten and brighten up. That's not meant to be a dismissal of the crushing weight that comes with clinical depression. The pain that comes from depression is real and can result in suicidal thoughts, cutting, and painful isolation. There is a real difference between simple negative thinking and clinical depression, and it is important that you speak with your primary physician to determine where you fall on the spectrum.

The good news, though, is that there's nothing wrong with *you*. Nothing. Let me say that again: There's nothing wrong with you! Remember the Truth? You are perfect just as you are. There are simply sections of your brain where the lights have been turned off and where the electricity isn't passing through. That's it. So many of my clients experience shame about their depression, or even if it's not clinical depression, they feel terrible about thinking negative thoughts when they're actually having a bad day. I've found that clients who are especially hard on themselves are people who work in the wellness world. Apparently, yoga instructors are simply *not allowed* to have a negative thought, or if they teach aspects of the Law of Attraction, they panic that every negative thought they think is attracting a disaster. So, let's clear those two up quickly.

You are allowed to have a negative thought if you're having a bad day. But see it for what it is. Our lives are dictated by the lens through which we look at it. If you choose to think more negative thoughts than positive ones, that's what your world is going to look like.

The same thing is true of the Law of Attraction. Whatever thoughts you think most predominantly will be the experiences you attract into your life most predominantly. So, one slip up of "I look so fat in this" doesn't mean 50 extra pounds are waiting around the corner doing a happy dance and finally have permission to pounce on your thighs. Especially if you catch it right away!

Remember when I taught you what I do earlier in the book? Whenever I recognize my mind just thought a lie—an untruth that if believed would move my life in a direction I don't want to go—I take a deep breath and say "Cancel, cancel" to remind myself that I didn't mean it and it isn't true. Then, I replace it with a thought that actually serves me. Something like, "My body is magnificent. Every day in every way, I feel better and better about how I look in this dress." All of those things are either true or could be becoming true. I don't say "Cancel, cancel, I look hot as hell and I drop two dress sizes every time I put this on." To my brain in that moment, that would be a tad far-fetched. Make sure your replacement thoughts are believable and that they support the vision and version of yourself you want to become.

Does this process mean you will magically drop 10 pounds right in the moment or never think a negative thought about yourself again after practicing it once? At this point, I think we've established the snake oil marketing has no place here. This process is a pattern interrupt. It weakens neurons that are firing from wiring together and making the old negative pattern stronger while strengthening the new, positive pattern. We interrupt the pattern with something that serves us, something that is true.

The Truth is, whatever the degree of negative thinking you may have experienced in the past, there's nothing wrong with you. Those sections of the brain where the power is out may be the result of an organic change in the brain or chemical makeup of the body. Or it could be programming you picked up from one of the Three E's, which we discussed earlier. It could have been the result of a trauma, diet, or a combination of all of the above.

You now know that hypnotherapy can help you tremendously in transforming the state of your thinking. When it comes to medication, you and your physician know the right steps for you, and you can always look into TMS and neurofeedback as well, which are powerful tools without any adverse side effects (more on this in Chapter 4).

## Stress/Anxiety

According to the Anxiety and Depression Association of America (ADAA), "Everyone experiences stress and anxiety at one time or another. The difference between them is that stress is a response to a threat in a situation. Anxiety is a reaction to the stress."[4]

This means we can be stressed without being anxious, but we can't be anxious without first being stressed. When we experience stress or both stress and anxiety, our brain flips into "autopilot" even more than normal. It begins to run almost completely on the big, thick, often-used neural highway of habits. This is because it takes *a lot* of energy to do something new, and when we're stressed, the body and mind are worried about surviving the perceived threat. This means it's all hands on deck. All available energy is hoarded for survival, which doesn't leave enough juice left over to create a new outcome. For example, "I'm stressed but am choosing not to smoke a cigarette" is not going to fly. The brain goes into autopilot so that it can save energy and use that energy to survive.

But stress doesn't just trigger our habits; stress itself has become a habit. We've spoken a lot about stress and anxiety in this book already because one of the most effective ways to reach the theta brain wave state is through deep relaxation. There are other ways to do it, such as confusion, loss of equilibrium, startling the client, and more insidious techniques, like torture. I use the relaxation technique more than the startling or loss of equilibrium techniques, which are popular in stage hypnosis, simply because the theatrics aren't necessary. Also, I want you to know that you're the one making this change. When you learn to relax yourself deeply into this theta brain wave state, there's no room to consider that perhaps it was because of the fancy way I dropped your arm or interrupted your sentence. You're the powerful one, and you're powerful enough to do this with the assistance of a trained professional or thorough self-hypnosis.

We're spending even more time on stress now because it's a habit that everyone in the western world has, and it's getting worse.

The more we feel stress, the more likely we are to feel it. Although there are some appropriate situations where a modicum of stress is understandable, it's in your best interest to stay as far away from a stress response as possible.

Here are two examples:

**Example A:** You're extremely stressed out because you have the biggest meeting of the year coming up. You've been preparing for weeks, and now, you'll be late because your car was just rear-ended. Luckily, no one was hurt, but now, you might miss the meeting altogether.

**Example B:** You're extremely stressed out while sitting in traffic every single day. There is nothing absolutely dire you have to do immediately following the exit off of the freeway, but you're banging your hand on the steering wheel, huffing and puffing, and making hand gestures that range from childish to obscene.

Example A is an appropriate stress response. Again, until we peel back the layers of conditioning further, we don't realize that even that wasn't a big deal or "a deal" at all. But for many who are still beginners and a long way from Nirvana, example A is perfectly normal. It happens rarely, and it makes sense.

Example B is never okay. It isn't an appropriate response to be that upset every day for the same thing and to blame everyone around you, who might also be blaming everyone around them. Think about it: it's ludicrous.

More and more people are stressed *all* the time. It's horrible to feel that way, and it's horrible for everyone else to be around. I genuinely believe if we could cut overall stress levels down by 30 percent, the world we live in would be unrecognizably beautiful. Stress gives us tunnel vision. It takes an already egomaniacal society and makes it even more about "me, me, me." I'm stressed, so the barista had better make my coffee *now*, faster, faster. I'm stressed, so I can be mean and say things I don't mean to my assistant/spouse/friend/stranger and take them back later.

On the other side of the situation is: "I'm stressed because my boss is too cheap to hire another barista, and now this woman is glaring at me. When I'm stressed, I make more mistakes with the order and have to start over. My boss is such an idiot. Let's see how stressed she is when I quit."

Somehow, we manage to believe our stress is more important than that of everyone around us. The truth is, we use stress as a way to express in desperation, "I'm important," and this, in turn, becomes an excuse for poor behavior. This is the opposite of taking responsibility.

For a fun little exercise, imagine that every time you feel stressed and act out because of it, that every single person you affected due to your stress is now just as stressed as you for reasons that are just as important as yours. Imagine this chain reaction throughout the world. Is this going to create the utopia of your dreams?

In other words, we need a collective message: Enough!

The beginner's tool is to learn to take responsibility and learn to break down the habit of stress. The advanced tool is to know that none of the stress is real anyway. The Truth is, giving into the stress habit further separates us from who we really are. It activates our limb topics and lends itself to behavior that's far below our best selves.

While the natural stress response to an actual threat may be useful every now and again, experiencing constant stress simply because our brain is used to doing so makes for an uglier world than we need to live in.

What about anxiety? For anyone who has ever experienced an anxiety or panic attack, you already know they're outright debilitating and certainly don't feel like a choice. Luckily, they can be reversed by using hypnotherapy. Then, the less you have them, the less likely you are to worry about having one, and the less likely you are to have one at all.

Luckily, all hypnosis helps to decrease stress and anxiety because that is the very act of accessing the theta state; feeling safe and relaxed. To decrease your stress and anxiety quickly, I recommend going back to the self-hypnosis process from Chapter 1 and practicing it or listening to it at www.CloseYourEyesGetFree.com back to back two or three times in a row. This will have a wonderfully compounding effect and you'll feel as if you had a mini vacation in no time at all.

# Root Topics

## Lack of Self-Confidence

Lack of self-confidence reveals itself through many different limb topics. Our career, relationships, sense of style, even the music we listen to or don't listen to can be a reflection of our self-confidence.

The beautiful thing about root topics is that they are a two-way street. If you were to go to Toastmasters (a group devoted to helping people learn to speak in public) to learn how to give a better speech, it might solve a fear of public speaking, but it wouldn't necessarily cure the root topic of lack of self-confidence. This would be chopping off a limb, but with the root topic still intact, another branch could very well grow in its place. If you were to simply fix the root topic of self-confidence during hypnotherapy, but then never give a speech for the rest of your life, the public speaking limb might never fully heal.

The sweet spot is when you take the time to heal the root topic on the subconscious level, while also taking tangible action on the conscious level. For example, combining hypnotherapy for lack of self-confidence with the experience of practicing public speaking on a regular basis at Toastmasters.

In my experience, lack of self-confidence stems from a few key events in childhood that blew themselves out of proportion. For me, it was tee-ball. I was so nervous waiting in line to hit the ball, I got up to bat and kept hitting the stick the ball was on. I heard a few people laugh, and that was it: The "I can't do it," "I'm not good at sports," "I hate sports" mantras began. I wonder what would have happened if I had somehow hit the ball out of the park. What would have happened if my first experience with sports had been an overwhelmingly positive one? My gym class experiences may have been very different for the next decade.

So, while my self-confidence in sports was destroyed right out of the gate, I didn't really care. I may not have developed a love of sports because I was embarrassed so early on, or I genuinely may not have cared enough in the first place to do a good job. We may never know because I don't feel the drive to improve that area of my life. The unfortunate thing is I also came to "hate" anything that looked at all like a sport. The idea of participating in a relay race or a game of charades makes me so nervous I can't even tell you. A group setting where other people depend on you to do well is not my jam. Whether it's extremely serious or ridiculous and playful, I'm out. "I can't do it, I'm not good at it, I'll just let you down."

So, although my rendezvous with sports may not have had any truly crushing impact on my life on the surface, that lack of self-confidence is insidious. I know that the fear of playing sports was the cousin to my fear of singing in public, and singing was something I loved from the start. I also didn't have any innate talent or singing ability when I was young. In fact, in a hypnosis session early on, I remembered a family member saying, "Who killed the cat?" when I was belting out a tune at around the age of eight. It was meant to be a joke because I was probably way out of tune. The person who said it had never wanted to be a singer and couldn't imagine I would either, but I did. During my first session to overcome my fear of singing, I remembered that moment, and my little heart was crushed. It felt just like I did when I couldn't hit the tee-ball.

Our subconscious mind lumps things together: bad experiences over here, good experiences over there; then it directs the conscious mind to go for more of the good, safe experiences and steer clear of the bad experiences. So, what happens when the bad experience is something you *love* or something that's a requirement for you to advance at your job, like public speaking or flying?

The point is that lack of self-confidence about *anything* colors our self-confidence about *everything*. I may never choose to play sports, but my avoidance of them and all public forms of "playing" has drained a lot of color from my life that could have been there.

Here is an exercise you can complete to see what kinds of connections your subconscious is making without your permission:

Think about things you just don't like to do and write them down on a piece of paper.

Circle any of those where you remember having had a bad or embarrassing experience as a child.

Ask yourself, could this experience have anything to do with why you don't like the other items on the list?

In what ways has the avoidance of each of these items impacted your life?

This book is called *Close Your Eyes, Get Free* because freedom is paramount—the freedom to play along with a silly game without being mortified the entire time, or the freedom to say "no, thanks" with a smile on your face and mean it just because you don't want to, not because you're afraid to.

Freedom comes when all options are available to us, when we're not limited to a few behaviors that happen to feel comfy. You don't have to want to do everything, but believing there is anything you *can't* do or aren't good at is a limitation that we simply don't need to have in life. While all of the self-hypnosis processes throughout this book will certainly lend a hand to increasing your self-confidence, you can also log in to www.CloseYourEyesGetFree.com and access a sample hypnosis recording all about this fundamental topic.

## Lack of Self-Worth

Lack of self-worth as a root topic often manifests itself in limb topics that are relationship-based. Lack of self-worth can also play into things like overeating and procrastination, but that usually takes a little bit of digging to get to, whereas lack of self-worth is always a common denominator when someone stays in an unhealthy relationship.

Many of us reading this live in a society where we're told we're capable of anything, that everything we do is fabulous (i.e., "participation trophies"), but simultaneously, we're told not to be full of ourself and not to brag or gloat.

The idea of authentic self-worth gets mucked up in this confusion. How can I believe I'm smart, beautiful, and capable when believing that would be narcissistic?

How can I know there's someone out there in the world who would treat me better than this, who wouldn't put me down, or lie to me, or hurt me? What if this is the best I'd ever get? Isn't this pain better than the fear of the unknown or, God forbid, being alone?

Self-worth comes from knowing you're just as good as everyone else, yet no better. This is such an antimillennial philosophy that it's a challenge for me to wrap my head around it sometimes, and I've been teaching these concepts to my students for years! While I was growing up, the predominant messages I heard were hard at work telling me how special I was, but don't brag; you can do anything, but stop being egomaniacal; you were born to be a leader, but don't be bossy.

Everything we learn growing up in school is by comparison. They got a 98 on the exam, and you got an 86. They're smarter than you. You ran the mile in five minutes, and they ran it in seven minutes. You're a better athlete. He makes $50,000/year, and she makes $300,000/year. The latter is "successful."

Take a deep breath, and consider what it means to be just as good as everyone else and no better. It means you are just as worthy of happiness as everyone else.

By knowing this to be true, it doesn't limit us. It doesn't automatically give the promotion to the other guy because even though everyone is just as good, worthy, and deserving as everyone else, only some people will do what it takes to get there.

Competition can be a force for bringing our best to the table, and it can create an atmosphere where the most creative solutions are produced. But far too often, it looks a lot more like a situation where there is always either a winner or a loser.

Our subconscious mind, in an attempt to keep us safe, will either have to put the other people down to defend the belief that we deserve to have more than them, or it will cause us to put ourself down so that we never enter into the arena. Either way, it's a lose-lose situation.

But the Truth is, you are worthy whether you win or lose!

A lot of people have a conscious fear that if they actually believe that they're worthy, no matter what, that they simply won't act; that somehow the lack of self-worth is a powerful motivator. To the contrary, I've found that my clients act infinitely more when their self-worth has improved. They believe they're worthy whether they win or lose, so the only "failure" would be to not try for something they truly want. If they get it, great. If they don't, they learned something and it was still a worthwhile experience.

## Lack of Self-Love

Both lack of self-confidence and lack of self-worth are derivatives of lack of self-love. If you loved yourself completely, you would naturally believe in yourself, take care of yourself, and be kind to others because there would be no perceived threat. If we have self-love, the nail-biting, phobias, insomnia, weight, and neuroses would melt away because the conduit trunk topics of anxiety, stress, and negative self-talk would cease to exist.

I realize this can all sound very "woo-woo" to anyone new to the topic, but truthfully, self-love couldn't be more practical for whoever wants to live their best life as the best version of themselves.

For example, let's say you have a fluffy golden retriever puppy with big paws and a goofy smile. His name is Sam, and you *love* this fur baby. Sammy can do no wrong! He may rip your shoes to shreds and more or less destroy the house in various ways, but after a moment of scolding or the hiring of a trainer, you go right back to loving Sam so much your heart could just burst. You want Sam to eat the very best food without grains or gross additives. You want to take Sam for walks simply because of the pep in his step and the way he wags his tail out of the pure need to express his love for the same walk he's taken a million times before. You want Sam to be groomed by someone who loves him as much as you do, you hate leaving him even when you're going on a fabulous vacation, and you genuinely believe he's the best dog in the world. But that doesn't mean you hate every other dog on the planet and hope they suffer and never get to play. Heck no, you love other dogs, too! You see their value, you see their cuteness, you love their unique personality, and you appreciate their people because you know they love their dogs as much as you love yours. Connection! Love! Appreciation!

Here's an important exercise: For just one day, love yourself as much as you love your dog (or cat or your favorite sports team— whatever floats your boat).

Do what makes your tail wag! Feed yourself only the best out of love. Forgive and forget in the same instant. Go for the ball, and wag your tail when you miss. Wag your tail when you catch it, and take a nap because they're great.

When you love Sam, you don't say, "I love you so much, so eat garbage. We're not going for a walk, and I don't care if you cry when I leave. Stop being such a baby. You can't do anything right." Quite the contrary, if anything, that love drives you to be the very best you can be for Sam.

That's what happens when you experience self-love. You want the best for yourself, because you know you're worthy of it and that others are worthy of it at the same time.

We can get closer to self-love by peeling away the layers of conditioning, but self-love doesn't need to be created. It already exists in pure form. Recognize yourself for what you truly are— perfect. If you want to boost your self-love starting today, move to the scripts on self-worth (Chapter 2) and gratitude (Chapter 3).

# Next Steps

Excellent! In this chapter you learned a little bit about a lot of the most common topics within hypnotherapy and you have completed the Break Through Procrastination self-hypnosis process on page 189!

- Now, go ahead and visit www.CloseYourEyesGetFree .com to access this chapter's hypnosis recording. Pop in your headphones, sit back, relax, and Close Your Eyes, Get Free.

- After you listen to the recording, please let me know how it went! Using the hashtag #CloseYourEyesGetFree on Instagram or Twitter, message me @GraceSmithTV your starting and ending numbers on the stress scale. Please also share with me the one root, trunk, or limb topic that will be most beneficial for you to overcome in your journey toward personal freedom. By using the hashtag, you'll get to see how other readers are improving right alongside you, plus I will have an opportunity to cheer you on!

- Move on to Chapter 10 and keep a lookout for all of the wonderful benefits you're no doubt experiencing as a result of learning the power of hypnosis.

# Chapter 10

# Serendipity

Colleen is a nurse; she has very fair skin, dirty blond hair, and big, green, catlike eyes. She works long hours on her feet. She holds hands with the dying, consoles family members, and cheers her patients on toward health. Over the years, as she became more confident in her work and as medical advancements continued to improve drastically, Colleen was happy to notice that in general, her patients were staying healthier longer with fewer complications. Overall health was on the rise over those thirty years for nearly everyone, it seemed . . . except for her.

While growing up, her mother had always scolded her, "You eat every meal like it's your last." No matter how much she had wanted to slow her pace or count her chews until she reached fifty before swallowing, she was always the first one done with her dinner. The difference was, while growing up, the food she ate was nutritious and well balanced. Once she got to the hospital, it was a different story.

It had started out as a harmless pattern. In the break room, there were always donuts, cookies, pies, and cupcakes. The patients' families would bake these treats to say "thank you," and it would have been rude not to accept. When you work on a busy floor, as she always had, finding the time to eat can be a challenge.

So, Colleen found herself regularly running into the break room and eating quite a lot in a short period of time. At first, it didn't appear like binge eating, but over time, a simple equation formed in the mind. It comprised of a stressful environment, lack of time to eat, and lots of delicious temptation all in one place. Eventually, the habit of eating a lot very quickly followed her home. It started with a few extra pounds here or there, which a successful diet would wipe out at first. But in a short period of time, twice as many pounds would return. By the time Colleen was approaching retirement, she was extremely overweight.

It had become very difficult for her to work. The extra weight, combined with all of those years of being on her feet, had made her knees very weak. She was in pain, she was tired, and she was ashamed. She felt that while advocating for the health and well-being of her patients, they were all noting the result of her less-than-healthy food choices and portion sizes over the years. She loved her work but she felt humiliated every day. To top it off, she was in need of double knee replacement surgery. However, due to her weight, the insurance companies would only cover a portion of the cost. The surgery would diminish her retirement account significantly. After all those years of service, she was terrified for her future.

Reluctantly, Colleen sought the help of a hypnotherapist for weight loss. She had tried every fad exercise from barre to Bikram to beach bod. She had tried every fad diet from no meat, to no gluten, to only if it fell from a tree, to everything wrapped in bacon. They all resulted in minimal short-term results and nothing long-lasting. She had tried traditional therapy, juice cleanses, and even acupuncture. For her very Western medicine–oriented mind, this was quite a stretch. But she was at her wits' end when she figured, "I've tried everything else, so what do I have to lose?"

She arrived at the hypnotherapist's office five minutes early, sat down in the waiting room, and crossed her arms over her chest. As much as she wanted this to work, she felt as if she was almost insulting her medical peers by being there. If the letters MD and PhD couldn't help her, how the heck was a CHt (certified hypnotherapist) going to help? After a few minutes, an assistant welcomed her to the office. It was comfortable, not too big, not too small, with soft lighting, a big comfy recliner chair, a desk, two office chairs, some plants, and (oh, brother) crystals. "What's next?" Colleen thought to herself. "A deck of tarot cards?"

In truth, Colleen was open-minded, but she was scared and so desperately wanted results that her nerves were shot. The cozy setting of this office was in such stark contrast to the sterilized, fluorescent lighting she was used to that her body didn't know whether to relax or run. Despite her inner dialogue, she had to admit that the hypnotherapist seemed nice and knowledgeable enough as the session began. They discussed Colleen's weight loss goal, her history, and her expectations for the session.

When they began, the hypnotherapist mentioned that they would be returning to the source of the issue to clear it up so that she could live a healthier life in the present moment. "Even when we go backward, it's all in service of the present," the hypnotherapist said.

Colleen replied, "Well, I know the source. It's the brownies back in the hospital break room."

The hypnotherapist smiled and agreed that those brownies very well could be the source, but there may also be an earlier experience, maybe, maybe not. "Simply keep an open mind, and we'll see what comes up."

Colleen agreed but had no idea what she was about to learn.

The beginning of the session started out as was to be expected, with deep relaxation and a safe place. When the hypnotherapist told Colleen to return to the source of the binge eating, something fascinating occurred. All of sudden, the nurse felt very, very hungry and very sad. She could tell she was still in the hypnotherapist's office, and she could still hear her voice, but she was also someplace else entirely. The hypnotherapist would ask questions about where Colleen was and what was happening, and the nurse would answer.

Hypnotherapist: "Look down where your feet might be. Take your time. Then, let me know what you notice."

Colleen: "I don't have shoes on. My feet are covered in dust and dirt. I'm a boy. I feel about twelve years old."

Hypnotherapist: "That's right. Your feet are covered in dust and dirt. You're twelve years old."

Colleen: "I have dark skin, very dark skin. Darker than my brother. He just died. I'm so sad. I can't believe he's gone." (Colleen starts crying hysterically.)

Hypnotherapist (in a soothing and understanding voice): "That's right. Your brother just died, and you can't believe he's gone. What happened to him?"

Colleen: "There wasn't anymore food, and he died, just died. I could hear them talking, saying he would be next. I didn't want to believe it, but then . . . (sobbing) I was carrying him. We were walking to find fresh water. He was looking at me. And then he was still looking at me, but he was gone."

As the session continued, they learned that the twelve-year-old boy lived in a village that had been attacked. All of their livestock had been killed, and many people were dying of starvation. Often, the youngest and oldest members of the family died first. The boy had lost his parents in the attacks, and his only remaining family, his little brother, was now gone. Later on in the session, the boy found a carcass of an animal and ate as if it were his last meal. *It was.*

Colleen: "I've been walking for two days since we found the zebra. I just saw myself fall down. I think I died. . . . Yes, I died."

Hypnotherapist: "That's right. Where are you now in relation to your body?"

Colleen: "I'm above it, looking down."

Hypnotherapist: "How do you feel?"

Colleen: "Free, happy to be free, but I miss my brother."

The hypnotherapist and Colleen continued to do healing work around the details of the session. Finally, when the hypnotherapist counted Colleen back up, and she emerged from the hypnosis, she said with tears in her eyes, "I don't know what that was, but I still miss my brother. And I'm an only child!"

From that day forward, Colleen never ate another meal as if it were her last.

## ··· WHAT THE HECK IS PAST LIFE REGRESSION? ···

You may be thinking, "Okay, Grace, I was with you through all of this. But, really, past life regression?" Stick with me here. A past life regression is a way of accessing memories from past lives through the use of hypnosis. I believe the most interesting thing about past life regressions is that you don't need to "believe" in them, or in past lives at all, to have this experience. In my mind, it's actually just as fascinating if past lives *aren't* actually real. It's pretty amazing that the mind could create such a detailed story about another life that we feel a deep emotional connection to and that we can actually *heal* from. I don't feel confident in saying that past lives are real or not because we can't know for sure.

However, after conducting many past life regressions myself with clients, I tend to lean toward the idea that they are real. The experiences are just so vivid and powerful. That said, I've had plenty of clients who firmly believe it's all a construction of the mind and go on to heal from their past life regressions (PLRs) all the same. Either way, this is a fascinating and powerful experience that I highly recommend.

Interestingly, spontaneous past life regressions can happen during purely clinical hypnotherapy sessions. This is well documented in both *Journey of Souls*, by Dr. Michael Newton (more on how this book forever changed the course of my life in just a bit) and the popular book *Many Lives, Many Masters*, by Dr. Brian Weiss. In my private practice, this has happened a few times, where the client comes to work with me on something rather "basic" and clinical. Yet, when I say "return to the source," all of a sudden, the details of their experience are clearly about another time in history, another location, and another person altogether.

One of the most popular stories of past life regression is the story of Chase Bowman, a young American boy who had an intense phobia of loud noises and complained of pain in his wrist at a very young age. Under hypnosis, Chase recounted accurate and chilling details of being a Civil War soldier who fought in some of the most horrific battles and was shot in the wrist. There is also the story of Barbro Karlen, who, at an early age, had a fear of showers and men in uniform. She started having spontaneous memories at the age of three, telling her parents that she was Anne Frank, who wasn't well known then because her diaries had not yet been published. These are two rather well-documented cases.[1]

Although lining up past life regression experiences with historical details to determine accuracy might be fascinating, it isn't why I'm interested in PLRs. For me, it's interesting because through these experiences, we have the capacity to heal and live more fully in the present moment.

Over a billion people in the world are raised to believe in reincarnation, so these ideas are really only shocking and surprising to a segment of the world's population. To the rest, it's perfectly normal. For example, when I was living in Brazil, I attended a Spiritist church ceremony that has a lot of similarities to Catholicism in terms of the saints they pray to and a direct connection to Jesus, but Spiritists also believe in past lives. The entire concept of karma depends upon a belief in reincarnation and bringing forth our karmic debt into our current lifetime. Hinduism, Buddhism, Jainism, and Sikhism have the concepts of karma and rebirth built into the very foundation of their beliefs. Hypnosis is not the only way but is certainly one of the most powerful ways to experience a past life regression.

· · · · · · · · · · · · · · · · · · · · · · · · · · · · · · · · · · · · · · · · · · · · · · · · · · · · · · · · · · ·

I want to congratulate you for making it this far. I can only imagine the wonderful benefits you're already experiencing from having given your time and energy to learning how to close your eyes and get free. At this point, you may be wondering about my journey and how I became a hypnotherapist. Let me be clear: There was never, ever, a time in my life when I thought I would be writing this book. I didn't grow up wanting to sit in cozy rooms with Himalayan pink salt lamps and Reiki frequency music while speaking to people who have their eyes closed.

My mother is an amazing physical therapist, so naturally, while choosing career paths, I never wanted to touch the word *therapist* of any kind with a 1,000-foot pole. In my mind, I took after my entrepreneurial father and was good at business, decent at the arts, and no good at all at helping others. Needless to say, this career came as a big surprise, and one that I'm now infinitely grateful for. My journey with hypnosis began when I had my own experience similar to that of Colleen, the nurse in our story; it was right after I hit rock bottom and booked my very first past life regression session as a result.

My first experience with high levels of stress began when I started working as an account executive for one of the world's largest fund-raising companies right after graduating from college in 2008. This was the peak of the financial recession, and working in fund-raising at a time when thousands of people were losing their jobs and retirement funds created a precarious situation, to say the least. Even with my proven success with fund-raising for Habitat for Humanity while in college, nothing prepared me for working on campaigns that were in the hundreds of millions of dollars.

Each day, as soon as my eyes opened, I felt an immediate sense of dread. Every cell in my body was resisting the day ahead. My heart would race with fear with each phone call or chime of an e-mail entering my inbox. I knew it would be one of my bosses following up on my numbers. The long days working in the trenches, so to speak, exacerbated the stress, not to mention I was philosophically opposed to just about everything about our client at the time. It just didn't feel right. My high hopes of truly making a difference through sophisticated, large-scale fund-raising were quickly replaced by an overwhelming anxiety that I had never encountered. I had never felt more incongruent in my life and had never felt so disappointed in myself.

At this point in my life, I hadn't learned any healthy coping skills for debilitating levels of stress, partially because I hadn't needed them and partially because "Stress Relief Class" isn't exactly an elective available in most high schools or colleges. The only wonderful part of this job was the friendships I made with the other young account executives. My method of managing my emotions was to party with my beloved co-workers after work, which often included excessive drinking. While most of my colleagues could manage their intake, before I knew it, I could barely make it to early morning sales meetings without being completely hungover. There was one morning in particular when I literally had to crawl on hands and knees out of bed and down the steps of my apartment to my computer, sick with pain and worry about remembering my numbers. With a throbbing headache, I was in the fetal position for the entire call, and as soon as the call was over I burst into tears. I was miserable.

When I finally left that position, I had high hopes that my new job would result in a more congruent way of existence, but no such luck. Back in New York, my partying was only getting worse. I was underperforming at my new job, I was always sick from a run-down immune system, I had put on weight and looked puffy and tired, and my personal relationships were a constant rotation of drama and upset. Still, somehow, I managed to convince myself that my drinking wasn't the problem.

On one random evening in early December 2010, while watching a movie at my Lower East Side apartment with a friend, I found myself rummaging through the kitchen for a drink. Eventually, at the back of the refrigerator, I spotted a Mike's Hard Lemonade, I immediately opened it and took a sip. "Ugh, this is disgusting!" I exclaimed, and then promptly continued drinking the yellow stuff. Why? Because earlier that night I had had wine with dinner and I was never able to stop drinking once I started; never in my life did I ever just have one drink.

My friend, who was by no means a saint, gave me a concerned look and said, "Why would you need to drink when it's just the two of us watching a movie? I think you might have a problem . . . I really think you might be an alcoholic." For some reason, that message, that day got through to me. I had heard it plenty of times before, and you'd think when an ex dumped me for being a complete idiot and breaking his trust in what seemed like three seconds into our awesome relationship, or when I broke my arm and couldn't exactly remember how, or when I called in "sick" to work for the billionth time knowing my job security was already on thin ice, that one of those moments would have done it. But, no, it was this quiet night at home that finally got through. My friend gave me a hug and left. I kept drinking.

After a few hours, the fact that I might actually have an issue had built up to a feverish crescendo in my mind. I was genuinely scared. Partying wasn't a *part* of my identity. As far as I was concerned, it *was* my identity. For years now I had felt like a superhero when I would come home from work and, as if I was stepping into a phone booth, would rip off my professional clothes, throw on my hipster gear, and boldly head out to the bars, ready to accumulate "epic stories." But now, during this quiet night alone in my apartment, it was dawning on me that alcohol, which I thought had been my superpower, might actually be my kryptonite. It was a terrifying truth to admit to myself.

After a long, dramatic, and miraculous night (perhaps I'll tell that story in my next book), I quit drinking and drugging and have been sober since that day.

During my first few months of sobriety, I had serendipitous encounters with strangers all over the city—people telling me about their years of sobriety without any prompting on my end. I'd be in line waiting for coffee, and the person next to me would strike up a conversation that led to a discussion about being sober. Another time, an unprompted conversation on the subway led to another sobriety conversation. It was as if all these angels were planted all over the city, who would remind me that everything would be okay just when I needed to hear it most. One day, a cab driver started discussing his sobriety of twenty-three years out of the blue and suggested a book called *Journey of Souls*, by Dr. Michael Newton. It's about finding one's purpose in life through past life regression. The driver shared that the book was fascinating and asked whether I believed in past lives. Without hesitation, I replied, "No."

For some reason that I can't explain, I took his recommendation and read the book. My sobriety had humbled me and I was now more open to trying anything and everything that could possibly help me. Even though I didn't necessarily believe in past lives or reincarnation, I was intrigued. Specifically, what resonated with me was the idea that before we were born we *chose* our lives and all of the tough lessons we would learn while living it. "Why would I choose to be an alcoholic and get sober at the age of twenty-four?" was a question I wouldn't mind finding out the answer to.

Before this cab ride, it had never occurred to me before that maybe I had chosen this experience for a reason. Maybe there was a path I couldn't quite see yet. Past life regression seemed to be a way to explore this foreign concept, so I made an appointment with Paul Aurand at the Holistic Healing Center in New York to see whether my purpose could actually be revealed through a past life regression.

As the session began, Paul spoke calmly and slowly, and before I knew it, I felt deeply relaxed, as I did at the end of a yoga class while in savasana. It wasn't a blackout. I knew where I was and could still feel the blanket. As he continued, I was guided back to my childhood. He asked me questions about where I was and what I was doing, and the answers I gave surprised me. These were things that I had not thought about for years, and some were things I didn't know that I knew. I was unaware of these memories. It was all very intriguing to me, and I couldn't explain why I was giving answers like these, but they felt powerful and deeply significant all the same.

Some memories triggered happy tears, and even though I knew I could, I had no desire to wipe them away because my body was in such a state of relaxation that all vanity had melted away. Mascara must have been streaming down my face, but I just didn't care. I was so entrenched in what was going on in my mind.

Next, we traveled back even further, and I found myself in Nepal. It was incredible; I've never been to Nepal in this lifetime, but I just knew I was there. What followed next was even more amazing. I won't share too many of the details here because that could fill another book in and of itself, but suffice it to say, by the end of the session, I felt I understood exactly why I had just been through the challenge of getting sober. My mind was blown.

At the end of our three-hour session, Paul was wonderful and supportive. As I was headed out of the office, he handed me a flier, saying, "I have a hypnotherapy training coming up, if you're interested." I thought it was bizarre that he would mention this to me rather than just recommend follow-up sessions. Right away, I declined and told him I was in sales, not counseling, but I thanked him for offering. "Why would I become a hypnotherapist?' I thought the entire cab ride home.

Needless to say, over the coming weeks, the idea of attending the training never left me. The training cost around $2,000, which I didn't have lying around to put toward a certification I didn't think I wanted. But a week before the training was about to begin, I received a bonus sales check for $1,998 . . . the signs were getting less subtle.

Luckily, I had a week's vacation, so I could take the hypnotherapy training course with Paul. I had just moved to Brooklyn and had to travel each day to Jersey City for the training. On the first day in class, it was clear I was the black sheep of the group. Everyone was either a healer, counselor, nurse, or in some other career designed to help people already. As we went around the room and introduced ourself, sharing why we were there, I honestly answered, "I don't know why I'm here. I work in sales as an account executive for an online marketing company." My confusion didn't seem to bother anyone, nor did it bother me. In my gut, I knew there was a reason why I was there but couldn't articulate it yet.

As the class progressed throughout the week, I could physically feel a sensation as if my forehead was expanding with information. All of the ideas about the subconscious mind, habits, and being in control of your thoughts were new to me, but I somehow simultaneously felt that I was being reminded of something I had always known.

During the first hypnotherapy session that I conducted that week in class, I knew immediately that there was nothing I had ever done before that felt so natural. Immediately, all the right things came out of my mouth as I spoke to the fellow student who was standing in as my "client," even though I had a long way to go in terms of becoming a proficient certified hypnotherapist, I knew this was something that I had an innate talent for.

That first week of class, I was partnered with another female student who wanted to focus her sessions on binge eating. We would work together for the week-long training and also eat meals together, which is where I watched her transform. I watched each day as her eating habits changed after having these sessions with *me*. It was absolutely amazing. The first hypnotherapy session I had ever done was with a student in that class, and she stopped binge eating!

I realized that I had never actually made a tangible difference in someone's life to that degree, not until that week of hypnotherapy training. The fact that I had spent some time with a woman and had listened to her long enough to really hear her, that I was able to say things to her when she was in a relaxed and safe place that transformed her subconscious mind to the point where a habit that had plagued her entire life stopped . . . well, I was hooked.

Two additional transformative results came about around the same time that I was wrapping up this training and becoming certified as a hypnotherapist, which cemented my belief in how powerful hypnosis could be for an individual. First, up to that point, I remained strong in my sobriety from drugs and alcohol, and luckily still have to this day, but I had not been able to stop smoking. Well, in just two sessions with Paul, I quit smoking and have been a nonsmoker ever since.

Second, I had a fear of singing in public even though I was passionate about singing. This fear kept me off the stage and out of the public eye from the time I had graduated from high school until I was twenty-five . . . seven years later. Also during my first certification training course, I was hypnotized to overcome my fear of public speaking and singing; within a few weeks, I was the lead singer of an all-girl rock band and I am now paid thousands of dollars to speak to large audiences. I can't imagine what my life would be like today without these breakthroughs.

My life had been truly transformed, yet I still hadn't fully embraced the idea of being a full-time hypnotherapist. I was still working at my job as an account executive and conducting sessions with friends, family, and a few word-of-mouth clients. Every single time I worked with someone, I was utterly amazed. It just wasn't getting old. And if anything, I was more astonished with every passing moment that the people I worked with were losing weight, overcoming their fear of flying, or healing relationships and falling in love for the first time in their life. I actually saw myself making the world a better place, and I saw people evolving into who they wanted to be. I saw the greatness they were capable of becoming.

Despite the daily miracles I was witnessing, it wasn't until I experienced the opening story I shared with you in Chapter 1, my session with my future father-in-law, Alexandre, that I knew I had found my calling. As someone who had taken continuing education classes in human rights studies and had always dreamed of making a positive impact on humanity on a large scale, I realized this was the most profound and effective tool for personal transformation I had ever seen . . . the only problem was, no one understood it. And so, it was through a series of serendipitous events that I became a hypnotherapist, and I've been on a mission to make hypnosis mainstream ever since.

## Summary of a Transformation

While I have hypnotherapy to thank for the vast majority of positive transformations and successes in my life, I would be remiss if I didn't discuss the two other components that continue to be equally as important in how I ended up here today. As this book is about getting free, I feel it's important that you know the exact formula that resulted in the incredible life I live today.

First, I got sober. Without this step, the hypnotherapy would not have been as effective, and honestly, I probably wouldn't have been open enough to try it in the first place. If you feel you may be struggling with an addiction (it doesn't have to be to alcohol), I've provided you with some additional help in the Resources section. Please take a look and know that you are not alone.

The next step in my transformation was, without a doubt, hypnotherapy. I continue to practice self-hypnosis on a daily basis and I can't imagine my life without it. So many anxieties, fears, bad habits, and negative thoughts are now gone that I can hardly believe there was ever a time when I lived with them.

The third and final piece was meeting my husband. My life blossomed when I met Bernardo. He is the greatest gift I've been given in this life, and yet, had I not gotten sober first and cleaned up my subconscious mind next, I honestly don't believe we would have even met. The universe would never have brought us together simply because I wouldn't have been in a place to honor or nurture such a pure connection, and I don't believe he would have been interested in me in the state I used to operate from. Our frequencies would not have matched up. One beautiful step in the right direction led to the next and the next. This is what I want for you, a healthy body, a pristine subconscious mind, and all of the successes, including the gorgeous human connections that can flourish under those conditions. This brings us to our final self-hypnosis process.

# Self-Hypnosis Process: Weight Loss

I suggest reading through the following directions two or three times before beginning so that you will be able to follow along easily. Remember, there are video tutorials and audio recordings available to you at www.CloseYourEyesGetFree.com that will help you to become a self-hypnosis pro in no time at all.

- Begin by making note of your starting stress level. 10 = a full-blown panic attack and 0 = zero stress, no stress at all, the most relaxed a person can possibly be. Remember this number.
- Sit in a comfortable chair and place your feet flat on the ground, rest your hands gently in your lap.
- With your spine straight but comfortable, take 4 deep, slow breaths, inhaling through the nose for 4 counts and exhaling out the nose for 8 counts.
- Close your eyes and imagine gentle roots growing from the bottom of your feet down into the center of the Earth, grounding you.
- Imagine a color you love flowing in through the top of your head, all the way through your body, out the bottoms of your feet, and down those roots, down into the center of the Earth.
- Bring all of your focus and awareness and attention to the palms of your hands. Perhaps you can feel your palms tingling, perhaps you can feel your heartbeat in your hands, perhaps you notice a sensation of expansion in your hands. Just notice and breathe for a few moments

(you can choose whatever length of time feels best, about 30 seconds is my personal favorite).

- With your eyes closed, count down from 10 to 1, saying "I am going deeper and deeper" after each number: Ten, I am going deeper and deeper. Nine, I am going deeper and deeper. Eight, I am going deeper and deeper. Seven, I am going deeper and deeper. Six, I am going deeper and deeper. Five, I am going deeper and deeper. Four, I am going deeper and deeper. Three, I am going deeper and deeper. Two, I am going deeper and deeper. One, I am going deeper and deeper . . .
- (Optional Step) Next, take a nice, deep letting-go breath, open your eyes, and, if you are comfortably able to do so, pick up this book or tablet and lift it up in the air so that your eyes, are reading at an upward diagonal angle. Simply find the line where a wall meets the ceiling in your home. That is approximately where you want the center of your book to be—this does not need to be exact. If you are looking up at a diagonal, you are doing this correctly. Read the following hypno-affirmations at this upward diagonal angle until you have memorized them: Every day in every way I am losing weight and feeling great. I chew every bite until only liquid remains. Food is fuel, I only put the highest quality fuel into my body.
- Once you have memorized the hypno-affirmations, put the book back down and rest your hands comfortably in your lap.
- With your eyes closed, repeat the following hypno-affirmations you just memorized either silently in your

mind or out loud, 10 times: Every day in every way I am losing weight and feeling great. I chew every bite until only liquid remains. Food is fuel, I only put the highest quality fuel into my body.

- Take another nice, deep, letting-go breath and with your eyes closed, imagine all of your weight loss goals have already been achieved. See, feel, and experience yourself glowing with health, and that you have more energy and feel more joy than ever before.

- Once you've spent 1–2 minutes imagining that you've already lost the weight from those parts of the body you desire to lose weight from, imagine the same color as before flowing in through the top of your head, all the way through your body, out the bottoms of your feet, and down those roots into the center of the Earth.

- Put a gentle smile on your lips, open your eyes, stretch your arms over the top of your head, and say, "Yes!"

- Notice your new number on the scale (remember 0 = zero stress, the most relaxed you can be) and congratulate yourself on how quickly you improved your state!

Here is a simple summary for the process in case you need to peek your eyes open at any point for a quick reminder:

- Notice starting stress level from 0 to 10.
- Take 4 deep, slow breaths.
- Grow roots.
- Color.

- Notice your palms.
- Count down from 10 to 1 saying, "I am going deeper and deeper" after each number.
- Hold the book on an upward diagonal angle to memorize the hypno-affirmations.
- Repeat the hypno-affirmations "Every day in every way I am losing weight and feeling great. I chew every bite until only liquid remains. Food is fuel, I only put the highest quality fuel into my body" 10 times.
- Imagine you've already lost all the weight you desire to lose.
- Smile while opening your eyes and say, "Yes!"
- Notice new number on the scale of 0 to 10.
- Congratulate yourself for improving your state so quickly!

# Next Steps

Excellent! You have completed the Weight Loss self-hypnosis process!

- Now, go ahead and visit www.CloseYourEyesGetFree .com to access this chapter's hypnosis recording. Pop in your headphones, sit back, relax, and Close Your Eyes, Get Free.
- After you listen to the recording, please let me know how it went! Using the hashtag #CloseYourEyesGetFree on Instagram or Twitter, message me @GraceSmithTV your starting and ending numbers on the stress scale.

By using the hashtag, you'll get to see how other readers are improving right alongside you, plus I will have an opportunity to cheer you on!
- Move on to Chapter 11, and in the meantime, look out for all of the wonderful benefits you're experiencing from the regular use of hypnosis.

# Chapter 11

# You're Free! Now What?

There once was a child who was born absolutely perfect. Take a nice, deep, letting-go breath, and know that this has been true more than 7 billion times in your lifetime. The child is perfect, like a flawless emerald, and this never changes. Over the years, the child is exposed to many different energies and experiences. Some experiences and energies shine a light on what's already perfect so that the world can see it brightly. But sometimes, experiences and energies add layers of dust to what is perfect.

This dirt can compact into layers, like caked mud, and the mud can become like cement. At a certain point, after enough painful experiences and energies, it can appear as though there isn't a flawless emerald at all; rather, a brick of concrete. Hard, rough, dull, and impenetrable. Only by focusing on what's true do the layers come off. Perhaps with a jackhammer at first, then an archaeologist's scraper, then a brush, then just the softest tissue to wipe away the tiny bits of dust. Through it all, the emerald is perfect and unchanged. Not a scratch!

Hypnosis doesn't create the emerald. It doesn't add to the emerald. It can't make the emerald bigger or more beautiful or worth more on the black market. It's already perfect. Perfect! All hypnosis does is take away the layers of untruths and the negative experiences and energies that covered up what's true. The truth is, you are perfect, always have been, and always will be. You are that perfect child, and so is everyone else you know.

How does your heart feel when you consider that? You're perfect exactly as you are, and so is everyone you know. Some people you know may be covered in more dust than others, or it may even be our own dusty eyes fogging up what's true. Imagine a world where we all see the Truth about one another? Imagine!

Let's imagine the perfect child is now eight years old, and her name is Amanda.

She liked to kick stones on the way back from the bus stop. In fact, she **loved** kicking her stones, she was immersed in it, she looked forward to it, and she thought about it sometimes throughout the day. She would kick them the entire way home. She could kick really long distances. It was just as impressive as it was frustrating for the other kids walking home with her. The kids said the sound was annoying, and the fact that she did it every day was annoying. But actually, what was most bothersome to them was that she was so much better at it than everyone else. They never said this to her, though. They had all grown up together and had an unspoken rule to be kind to one another.

One day, however, someone snapped. One of the kids tried out for the soccer team and didn't get picked. He was mortified, but acted tough. Secretly, he couldn't stand the idea of Amanda kicking the stones all the way home after such an embarrassment, so he started talking about her on the bus. All too easily, the others joined in. They made a plan that seemed so funny to start kicking all of the stones as soon as they got off the bus so that there wouldn't be any left for Amanda. There was one kid who didn't want to play along, but they started teasing him, singing songs about trees and k-i-s-s-i-n-g. So, he turned red and gave in.

The day the kids ran down the street, laughing wildly, kicking all of the stones and leaving Amanda standing there watching them fade into the distance, was a day when a lot of dust was added to a lot of emeralds. Amanda stopped trusting her friends. She developed insecurities. She stopped kicking stones. She stopped taking chances publicly for fear of ridicule. The boy who didn't want to play along went against his morals, betrayed someone he cared about deeply, gave into peer pressure, and was ashamed. The children who were scolded by their parents for being a bad friend accumulated some dust, too. The boy who didn't make the soccer team added a lot of mud to his emerald.

Is this to say that Amanda will grow up to be a destitute failure? Not at all. But she stopped kicking stones, and she loved kicking stones. Will these other children end up in jail for having teased her? No. But they've found a way to rationalize meanness, which dulls and dims the light of everyone involved.

To show your bright, clean, sparkling emerald in this world of dusty blocks of concrete is your sole charge. We don't blame the little boy who didn't make the soccer team for all of the troubles in the world. We evaluate when we've been that little boy, and we take it upon ourself to cultivate healthy coping mechanisms. We resolve to be kinder. We notice the stones we've stopped kicking and ask ourself why? Why allow that dust to settle? In a world where we're free, truly free, there is no more "You did this." There's only "I did this." As individuals, we're the only ones who can make a difference—only us, all of us, one at a time.

# Close Your Eyes, Get Free

Let's recap all you've learned:

- Although hypnosis is not magic, it could very well be the most powerful and cost-effective tool for personal transformation that is available to us.
- Hypnosis is not sleep, a blackout state, mind control, or anything Hollywood has portrayed.
- Hypnosis is meditation with a goal.
- Thomas Edison used hypnosis to increase his problem-solving ability and to increase his creative thinking. We can do the same.
- The most important thing for you to remember is that you're the one with the power. No peace, growth, understanding, or enlightenment comes from anyone or anything external. A trained hypnotherapist may be able to guide you through processes they know have worked well with others before you, but you're the one making the change. You're the one transforming.

The purpose of this book is very simple. I want everyone to know that the powerful, transformative nature of hypnotherapy is available to them. I want you to know that hypnotherapy can work for you because everyone can be hypnotized. I want as many people as possible to seek out hypnotherapy *first* instead of turning to it as a last resort. I want everyone to stop equating one of the most powerful tools for transformation with chickens and stage show buffoonery. Every person who has told me "I can't be hypnotized" or "I don't believe in that stuff" or "I'll stick to meditation because I don't want you to control my mind" is a person who is likely stressed out more than necessary and who is holding on to more root, trunk, and limb issues than necessary. We all deserve to learn how to close our eyes and get free.

There are a number of different ways you can approach the use of hypnotherapy. I personally have found that although one-on-one sessions are the most powerful (so long as your hypnotherapist is well trained with plenty of experience and you have a great rapport with him or her), individual sessions tend to be expensive and aren't always convenient. Sometimes, I need to change my mind-set *right* this second. I get a phone call, text, or e-mail that, without a strong reframe, could throw off the rest of my day. My hypnotherapist (yes, I have an hypnotherapist!) isn't always available at the drop of a hat! So, I wanted to create something that would give everyone access to their subconscious mind anytime, anywhere.

To reach as many people as possible, I needed to make hypnosis accessible at a price that nearly anyone could afford. Private hypnotherapy sessions range from $100 to $1,000 per session, and at the time of this writing, insurance doesn't yet fully cover it, making what I've said repeatedly about having as many sessions as you need a nice thought, but a challenge for many.

That's how Grace Space was born. It's the world's number one library of hypnotherapy courses and recordings. Our community is growing rapidly, and I'm incredibly proud of the transformations our Grace Spacers experience on a daily basis. If you've logged into www.CloseYourEyesGetFree.com, you've already had a taste of all that Grace Space has available. If you haven't yet, be sure to visit www.gshypnosis.com to learn more.

Now that you've learned how to Close Your Eyes and Get Free, you have one simple homework assignment: Keep it up! The only way to continue benefiting from the use of hypnosis is to continue using it. Just like everything else you make a major priority, hypnosis needs to happen regularly. Remember: Neurons that fire together wire together. If you've been listening to the recordings that are paired with this book, you've already seen tremendous transformation to your overall mind-set and state of well-being. I'm sure of it. To maintain these, you must continue this practice and make it a habit. Make listening to a hypnosis recording a part of your day every day. You'll find that you are keeping your subconscious mind in shape as you move forward toward the life of your dreams.

It was my honor to share this information with you, and I hope now that you will join me in my mission of making hypnosis mainstream by purchasing a copy of this book for your loved ones so that they can learn to close their eyes and get free alongside you.

Remember, even though this book teaches self-hypnosis, everything you learned here was truly a process of *de*-hypnosis. You are already perfect just as you are, we are not adding anything, we are simply peeling away layers of conditioning that no longer or have never served you. The more you use hypnosis, the deeper the healing effects go and the longer they last, so keep it up. Know that a better world begins with you and is impossible without you. Every time you take responsibility for your actions, thoughts, and subconscious beliefs you are taking a step in the direction of a better life, the life of your dreams, and in doing so, you are giving everyone around you permission to do the same. It has been such an honor spending this time with you. I am so incredibly proud of you and the progress you have made. Please know, this is only the beginning. With love, Grace.

# List of Hypnotherapy Topics

# Resources

## Interested in working with me?

I look forward to it! Please visit www.gshypnosis.com to learn more about my private HypnoCoaching sessions, corporate retainer options, and speaking fees.

## Interested in finding a hypnotherapist near you?

When choosing a hypnotherapist, please make sure the person is certified with a minimum of a 250-hour program from a reputable instructor within a reputable association, such as IACT (www.hypnosisalliance.com/iact/iact_find_a_practitioner_form.php), NGH (ngh.net/referrals/request-form/), or IHF (hypnosisfederation.com/directory-user-listing/).

Additionally, a number of the students who graduated at the top of their class from my Grace Space Hypnotherapy School offer phone sessions and can work with you from anywhere in the world. If you would like to work with a hypnotherapist who was personally trained by me, you can book your sessions by visiting www.gshypnosis.com.

## Interested in becoming a certified hypnotherapist?

There is no other way to say it: becoming a hypnotherapist is incredibly rewarding. Whether you would be adding the skill of hypnotherapy to an existing practice or launching a brand-new career, I commend you for your interest in helping others Close Their Eyes and Get Free! Grace Space Hypnotherapy School is my 250+–hour certification course that includes both online and in-person components. At the time of writing this, my students hail from all over the world, including the USA, Germany, Estonia, Costa Rica, and the Cayman Islands. Upon successful completion of all coursework and exams, my students are certified by IACT (the International Association of Counselors and Therapists), among other associations, should they choose to register with more than one. I look forward to seeing you in class! For more information, visit www.gshypnosis.com.

## On Sobriety and Addiction

I want to take a moment to revisit what we discussed in Chapter 10 about addiction. Consider how learning to play an instrument may be anything but joyful in the moment when you're learning a new scale, but the ability of being able to create music for the rest of your life is a source of endless joy. Taking six shots to celebrate something might seem fun in the moment, but it's going to suck later on. Not just the next morning, but when the body, liver, skin, and brain begin to break down from all that poison over time. Take a moment now to examine your regular behaviors and ask yourself whether your habits tend to favor long-term joy or long-term pain. If you're leaning toward long-term pain, read on.

A lie we've been told repeatedly is that alcohol is fun, less dangerous than drugs (as evidenced in the fact that marijuana is illegal in most states and yet alcohol is sold at my local farmers' market, the movie theater, and Chuck E. Cheese) and that life without alcohol is "boring" and "uncool." Except for that, according to the

NIAAA, globally, alcohol misuse is the fifth leading risk factor for premature death and disability. Among people between the ages of fifteen and forty-nine, it is the *number one* leading risk factor for premature death and disability.[1]

There are two reasons I'm spending time on this: (1) I believed the lie; I spent over $1,000/month on alcohol in NYC (albeit not that hard to do even without an issue, when a martini is $14); I danced all night, went to parties in lofts, had scandalous stories to tell later . . . in short, I get it. I wanted to be cool and I believed for a long time that drugs and alcohol were a mandatory part of that persona. (2) This book is about freedom, how to get free from the things that are holding us back from living our best life. If you have a sneaking suspicion that alcohol, or any other form of addiction, is keeping you from living your best life, please know that you're in good company and you can break free from this.

The good news is that fewer people are drinking—sobriety is becoming cool! My friend Andrea Rice wrote an article called "It's Hip to Be Sober"[2] that went viral; Google it—it is an awesome and inspiring read. In summation, if you're regretting your decisions after a few glasses of something, on any kind of regular basis, before you even hope to see a smidgen of what hypnotherapy can do for you, I lovingly suggest that you hop on the gravy train and get hip with sobriety.

This does not mean hypnotherapy can't help you achieve sobriety; it can! But investing in hypnotherapy because you want to stop biting your nails or lose weight when overindulging is still on the schedule eight days a week is honestly just not the best use of your time or money. My advice? Switch your priorities around, break through the addiction first, then the sky is truly the limit.

Need help? You're not alone. According to the NIAAA, approximately 17 million adults in the United States aged eighteen and older had an AUD (alcohol use disorder) in 2012. Adolescents can be diagnosed with an AUD as well. Visit www.niaaa.nih.gov and www.aa.org for help today. While alcohol was my primary vice, this section applies to anything you may be abusing: food, drugs, credit card limits, and so on. Google support groups for your particular vice and prepare to learn how good it feels to be truly free.

# Appendix:
# The Power of Hypnosis

**Details of the study conducted in partnership with Dr. Keerthy Sunder and Samantha Franklin of Mind and Body Treatment and Research Institute and Grace Smith**

I told you a bit about our study in Chapter 4; as a reminder, over one hundred people started the study, and thirty-five people completed it from beginning to end. We used only data from those who completed the study. The study included listening to the same hypnosis recording once per day for seven days in a row and completing a quiz before and after. We measured twenty-one positive emotions and forty negative emotions, as well as overall stress levels. We chose these emotions based on commonly used words during therapy sessions and intake forms. The answers were randomized so that every time the quiz was taken, the answers were in a different order.

**The 21 positive emotions were:**

| | |
|---|---|
| Amazed | Driven |
| Calm | Eager |
| Comfortable | Energetic |
| Content | Excited |

Happy
Hopeful
Inspired
Intelligent
Joy
Loving
Motivated

Peaceful
Proud
Relaxed
Relieved
Satisfied
Smart

**The 40 negative emotions were:**

Angry
Annoyed
Anxious
Ashamed
Bitter
Bored
Confused
Depressed
Disdain
Disgusted
Embarrassed
Envious
Foolish
Frustrated
Furious
Grieving
Hurt
Inadequate
Insecure
Jealous

Lazy
Lonely
Lost
Miserable
Nervous
Overwhelmed
Procrastination
Resentful
Sad
Scared
Self-conscious
Shocked
Stupid
Suspicious
Tense
Terrified
Trapped
Uncomfortable
Worried
Worthless

With participants responding to fourteen different surveys (two per day for seven days), each with 61 data points, we had a lot of ground to cover. So, we brought in Eugene, a PhD data scientist and quantitative researcher, to help us sort through the data. Overall, the results were astounding. We found a dramatic increase in positive emotions and an even more dramatic decrease in negative emotions. To view the entire report, log into www .CloseYourEyesGetFree.com bonus material section, and we'll cover just the highlights here.

Out of thirty-five qualified initial participants only eighteen respondents completed the tasks correctly exactly two times a day for seven days. We measured the difference between pre- and post-treatment responses to each of the questions as well as long-term benefits. When measuring the long-term benefits, we compared the first data entry to the thirteenth rather than the fourteenth so that we could ascertain the long-term effect rather than the effect directly after listening to the recording. Although we saw improvements in the positive columns across the board, the biggest increases showed that on average participants were 32 percent happier, 29 percent more content, and 27 percent more satisfied after seven days of listening to the hypnosis recording. Decreases in negative emotion were even more significant, which is interesting. It appears it is faster to let go of a habit than to create one. At the same time, participants felt on average 80 percent less disdain, 80 percent less furious and disgusted, 58.8 percent less depressed, and 54.5 percent less angry, and the feeling of procrastination decreased by 51.5 percent. In addition, although stress levels decreased dramatically immediately following the recording, stress levels were still lower than ever by the end of the week. How much did overall stress levels decrease by in just seven days? Forty-five and a half percent. How would you like to be 45.5 percent less stressed out, 32 percent happier, and 51.5 percent less likely to procrastinate in just seven days? Amazing, isn't it? This qualitative data confirmed what my clients have always reported back, their success with hypnosis is dramatic, rapid, and lasting.

This table shows the top three increases and top three decreases after seven consecutive days of listening to the same hypnotherapy recording.

| Happy | + 32% |
|---|---|
| Content | + 29% |
| Satisfied | + 27% |
| Depressed | -58.8% |
| Angry | -54.5% |
| Procrastination | -51.5% |

This graph shows the immediate decrease in stress after listening to the recording as well as the long-term decrease of stress over time.

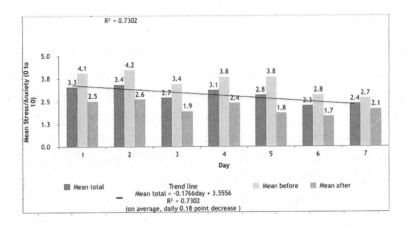

The extra-special good news? You have access to the same exact recording the participants in our study listened to every day for seven days so as to experience the results you've just read about. Why not take a moment now to log into the www.CloseYourEyes GetFree.com bonus section and listen to this recording? The more you listen, the deeper it goes, and the longer it lasts.

# Acknowledgments

There are so many wonderful souls who have poured their time, talent, and energy into making this book what I hope will be a source of both inspiration and transformation for all who read it.

From the bottom of my heart, thank you . . .

Lisa Gallagher, you have been with me from the very beginning, guiding me, supporting me, and ultimately seeing me through the accomplishment of one of my greatest goals. Thank you!

Renée Sedliar, for taking a chance on me and being so enthusiastic about our work together. I have loved working with you! To Amber Morris and everyone else at Da Capo Press who worked tirelessly to make this manuscript the best it could possibly be.

Carol Leggett, for helping me to bring the power of hypnosis into the homes and hearts of thousands of people I would not have otherwise reached. Having you in my corner makes me feel invincible; I am so grateful for all that you have done and continue to do.

To my family, friends, colleagues, and fellow authors who I leaned on heavily and who supported me throughout the writing of this book, including my wonderful brothers Ryan and George, my sister-in-law Nadia, Aunt Cindy and Uncle George, Mikaela Gauer, Jovanka Ciares, Danny Johnson, Gala Darling, Melanie Votaw, Amber Skye Noyes, Andie Gabrielson, Carrie Hammer, Melissa and Marise Cipriani, Rebekah Borucki,

Michelle, Ali and the entire Soul Camp Family, and so many more, thank you.

Patrick, when this book was first being written, you were only an idea in my mind, but by the time it is published, you will be five months old. Thank you for keeping me company with your gentle kicks and stretches today as I put these final touches on my first book. I cannot wait to support you in accomplishing your dreams! I love you.

Bernardo, you are an angel walking among us and everyone who knows you is lucky to share a glimpse of your enlightened existence. I am the luckiest. Thank you for being my partner in all things. *Eu te amo.*

Mom and Dad, you've always supported me, you've always loved me, you've always told me I could accomplish whatever I put my mind to. You are why I am able to share this message with others. Thank you!

Nana, for saving my "Smith Family News" clippings, for always saying I would be a writer, and for being so vibrant and amazing at one hundred years old that you got to see it come true!

Sweets, Zen, and Kona for constantly providing unconditional love and cuteness overload.

All of my mentors,

All of my phenomenal hypnotherapy students,

All of my clients and customers,

Every member of our incredible Grace Space community,

Thank you for joining me in my mission to make hypnosis mainstream.

I am so grateful.

# Notes

### Chapter 1. Freedom Begins in the Mind

1. Some states do not allow the term hypnotherapist unless the practitioner is also a board-certified clinical therapist, which often means that professionals trained as hypnotherapists use the terms hypnotist or "Hypno-Coach" for legal purposes.

### Chapter 2. How Our Habits Were Formed

1. For another real-life example of how one of my clients used hypnosis to overcoming nail-picking, take a look at this article by *Glamour* magazine: https://www.glamour.com/story/how-to-stop-biting-nails-hypnosis.

2. http://thoughtmedicine.com/2011/06/brain-wave-basics-what-you-need-to-know-about-states-of-consciousness/.

3. Ibid.

4. https://www.psychologytoday.com/blog/sold/201406/subliminal-ads-unconscious-influence-and-consumption.

5. Stephanie Castillo, "How Habits Are Formed, and Why They're So Hard to Change," *Medical Daily*, August 17, 2014, accessed August 30, 2016, http://www.medicaldaily.com/how-habits-are-formed-and-why-theyre-so-hard-change-298372.

### Chapter 3. The History of Hypnosis

1. https://en.wikipedia.org/wiki/James_Braid_(surgeon).

2. https://www.youtube.com/watch?v=MhFG3pZyu50.

3. http://www.oncologynurseadvisor.com/general-oncology/uses-of-hypnosis-to-treat-cancer-patients/article/631055/.

4. Les Brann and Jacky Owens, *The Handbook of Contemporary Clinical Hypnosis* (West Sussex, UK: Wiley-Blackwell, 2015), 33–34.

# Notes

5. "Mesmeric Amputation," *Journal of Practical Medicine* 75 (January 1, 1843): 280–282.

6. David Simons, Cath Potter, and Graham Temple, *Hypnosis and Communication in Dental Practice* (Surrey, UK: Quintessence, 2007).

7. Ibid., 9.

8. Freud 1889; cited in A. Gauld, *A History of Hypnotism* (Cambridge, UK: Cambridge University Press, 1992).

9. Ibid., 11.

## Chapter 4. The Science of Hypnosis

1. "The Neuron," BrainFacts, published April 1, 2012, accessed August 30, 2016, http://www.brainfacts.org/brain-basics/neuroanatomy/articles/2012/the-neuron/.

2. "Neurofeedback Treatment," Mind and Body Treatment and Research Institute, accessed August 30, 2016, https://mindandbodytreatment.com/pages/neurofeedback-treatment.

3. "TMS Treatment," Mind and Body Treatment and Research Institute, accessed August 30, 2016, https://mindandbodytreatment.com/pages/tms-treatment.

4. "The Evolutionary Layers of the Human Brain," The Brain from Top to Bottom, accessed August 30, 2016, http://thebrain.mcgill.ca/flash/d/d_05/d_05_cr/d_05_cr_her/d_05_cr_her.html.

5. Alfred A. Barrios, "Hypnotherapy: A Reappraisal," *Psychotherapy: Theory, Research and Practice* 7, no. 1 (1970): 5.

6. D. Spiegel and J. R. Bloom, "Group Therapy and Hypnosis Reduce Metastatic Breast Carcinoma Pain," *Psychosomatic Medicine* 45 (1983): 333–339.

7. D. Spiegel, J. R. Bloom, H. C. Kraemer, and E. Gottheil, "Effect of Psychosocial Treatment on Survival of Patients with Metastatic Breast Cancer," *Lancet* (1989): 888–891, https://www.ncbi.nlm.nih.gov/pubmed/2571815.

8. Carol Ginandes and Patricia Brooks, "Hypnosis Helps Healing," *Harvard Gazette*, published May 8, 2003, accessed August 30, 2016, http://news.harvard.edu/gazette/2003/05.08/01-hypnosis.html.

9. V. Miller, H. R. Carruthers, J. Morris, S. S. Hasan, S. Archbold, and P. J. Whorwell, "Hypnotherapy for Irritable Bowel Syndrome: An Audit of One Thousand Adult Patients," *Alimentary Pharmacology & Therapeutics* 41, no. 9 (May 2015): 844–855, accessed August 30, 2016, http://www.ibshypnosis.com/IBSresearch.html.

## Chapter 9. The Root, Trunk, and Limb:
## Overcoming Procrastination, Overeating, and Other Common Issues

1. http://www.cbsnews.com/news/the-staggering-cost-of-procrastination/.

2. https://www.cancercouncil.com.au/31899/uncategorized/a-brief-history-of-smoking/.

3. Nikki Tucker, October 1, 2012, http://www.medicaldaily.com/nail-biting-may-be-sign-obsessive-compulsive-disorder-242845.

4. "Stress," Anxiety and Depression Association of America, accessed September 4, 2016, https://www.adaa.org/understanding-anxiety/related-illnesses/stress.

## Chapter 10. Serendipity

1. Alex Matsuo, June 20, 2014, http://www.therichest.com/rich-list/most-shocking/10-most-shocking-cases-of-past-life-memories/.

## Resources

1. https://www.niaaa.nih.gov/alcohol-health/overview-alcohol-consumption/alcohol-facts-and-statistics.

2. http://wanderlust.com/journal/its-hip-to-be-sober/.

# Index

267

Barrios, Alfred A., 100
beauty, media and concept of, 47
Becker, Anne E., 45–46
Bernheim, Hippolyte, 66
beta brain waves (consciousness), 32,
    38, 92, 151–152
Bien, George, 73
binge eating, 222, 224
blame
    stress and, 210
    taking responsibility for actions
      and, 117–123
Bowman, Chase, 226
Braid, James, 62–63, 65, 66
brain
    adaptiveness and plasticity of,
      89
    defined, 88
    limbic, 97–99
    neocortex, 97–99
    reptilian, 89–90, 97–99
    sections of, 97–99
brain waves, 92–93
    alpha, 38, 92, 93, 152
    beta, 32, 38, 92, 151–152
    defined, 88
    delta, 21, 32, 38, 92, 93, 152
    gamma, 92
    infra-low, 92
    measuring, 89, 92
    theta (*see under* theta brain wave)
breast cancer, hypnotherapy and pain
    reduction in metastatic, 100
British Society of Medical and Dental
    Hypnosis, 72

Calvin (client story; anxiety), 165–167
change
    conditioned behaviors in
      subconscious mind,
      148–149
    desire to create, 148
Changkakoti, Sarojini Alva, 73
Chaplin, Charlie, 134

Charcot, Jean-Martin, 66
childhood
    formation of subconscious beliefs
      in, 152–153
    lack of self-confidence in
      adulthood and experience
      in, 213–214
childhood development, 37–40
Christianity
    mesmerism and, 65
    sleep temples and natural healing
      techniques and, 64
chronic worry, Susan's story, 127–130
cigarettes, addiction to, 153–154
Colleen (client story; weight loss),
    221–225
color, imagining in self-hypnosis, 102,
    104–105
communication on conscious *vs.*
    subconscious level, 110–111
competition, lack of self-worth and,
    216
complaints, 136
    self-hypnosis process to stop,
      139–141
conditioning, 34
    weight loss and, 198–199
conscious desires, aligning with
    subconscious beliefs, 149
conscious mind
    daily affirmations and, 130–131
    domains of, 9
consciousness (beta brain waves), 32,
    38, 92, 151–152
cortisol, stress reaction and, 23
cost
    of hypnosis recording, 16
    of private hypnotherapy sessions,
      16, 197, 247
    of self-hypnosis, 16
counting down, in self-hypnosis,
    24–25, 26–27
creativity, Edison's hypnotic state
    and, 84